F FOR FISH

HEALTH
RIGHT

F FOR FISH

Anne Williams

J. M. DENT & SONS LTD
London and Melbourne

First published 1987
© Anne Williams, 1987

This book is set in 11/12pt Linotron Goudy by
Gee Graphics Ltd
Made in Great Britain by
Mackays of Chatham for
J. M. Dent & Sons Ltd
Aldine House, 33 Welbeck Street, London W1M 8LX

British Library Cataloguing in Publication Data

Williams, Anne
    F for fish.———(Healthright)
    1. Fish as food
    I. Title   II. Series
    641.3'92   TX385

ISBN 0-460-02476-0

Contents

Acknowledgments

The section where an author pays tribute to those who have inspired and supported her throughout the writing of a book is often the part the reader skips over. Yet in cookery in particular it is important for author and reader to recognize the vital role played by others in the shaping of ideas, continuation of tradition and the inspiration to create and develop new dishes.

My culinary training, started by my mother who was a practical and consistently good cook, was continued by a Cordon Bleu course — a currently unfashionable cuisine whose emphasis on rather fussy dishes was all too often centred around ingredients that we, being more aware of the effect of diet on long-term health, wish only to consume in moderation. It did however provide a sound grounding in the theory and science of cooking — why things work, why they fail and what to do to achieve one and avoid the other.

Extensive travels through Europe, the Caribbean and Latin America opened my eyes to different ingredients and cuisines. Avid reading of a wealth of British writers — Elizabeth David and Jane Grigson of course, but also Marika Hanbury-Tennison and Theodora Fitzgibbon — educated me in the delights of good food, produced and eaten at home. My journalistic work as a restaurant critic has developed my critical awareness as well as giving further inspiration.

In connection with this particular book on fish, I would like especially to thank Brian Portch and his staff at the Chiswick branch of his three-shop wet fish empire. Brian is the ideal fishmonger, courteous, helpful, knowledgeable and a real fish enthusiast. He trains his staff to be likewise.

Lastly, I should like to thank my friends, particularly David Harsent, who have eaten their way through this book with enthusiasm and constructive criticism, and encouraged me tirelessly when my spirit was keen but my body flagging.

DIVING IN

Introduction

For a nation surrounded on all sides by water, we in Britain have until recently been astonishingly reluctant to include fish as a major part of our diet. You are more likely to find Scottish scampi in Portugal than Scotland, most of the catch from Cornwall's fishing fleets is exported to France, even the cheap and versatile herring is often shunned because of its bones.

Recently all that has begun to change. A growing public awareness of the effects our diet has on our health, coupled with the continuing rise in the price of meat, mean more and more people are turning away from Britain's traditional fare of roast beef and chops. Fish and poultry are without doubt better for you as a source of protein than red meat, especially fatty meats like belly of pork, breast of lamb or sausages which, being the cheapest cuts of meat, are what many people turn to when prices rise.

I decided to write this book because I found everybody I knew was wanting to eat fish more often, yet was frustrated by the lack of information about how to identify, deal with and cook the different varieties. The recipes here are very much aimed at the average cook, who may not have the time or inclination to spend too long at the stove, yet despite that enjoys cooking and serving good food.

We are all becoming more health-conscious, realizing that we should avoid too many saturated fats and cut down on consumption of cream, cheese, full-fat milk and butter. At the same time we are creatures of habit as well as enjoying tastes evolved by our past and most of us have no desire to revolutionize completely our choice of food. Moderation is the key. In some recipes here I have shown you how to make a dish using delicious fromage frais (fermented skimmed milk) instead of full-fat cream cheese but in others a spoonful or two of single cream is included in a soup. I have minimized the amount of salt and sugar, yet stuck with white flour rather than wholemeal where I feel it obtains a better result (in pastry-making for example), and sometimes suggested white rather than brown rice for the same reason. Likewise, I have recommended the use of small amounts of butter in preference to margarine where it seems to me that this markedly improves the flavour of the finished dish. Anybody who is eating fish three or four times a week instead of red meat has a head start on most of the population anyway, so you can enjoy the odd spoonful of cream or butter quite guiltlessly.

Of course, if you wish it is always possible to substitute the wholefood alternatives. I give some advice on flour in the section on sauces at the end of the book, and in the case of brown rice you will need to adjust the timing, as brown takes longer to cook. For the more delicate kinds of fish, it may be a good idea to sieve wholemeal flour, which will remove most of the bran and make the dish less heavy, or use 81 per cent wholemeal, and you can now even buy wholemeal puff pastry ready made.

The recipes in this book are arranged in three sections. The first, 'Swimming Along', deals with the kinds of fresh fish available in most fishmongers and good supermarkets — mackerel, trout, herring, red and grey mullet, mussels, squid and so on. The recipes are suitable for everyday meals, be they family casseroles or simply baked or grilled dishes which are quick for the single person to prepare. None of the ingredients is very expensive, nor is the preparation complicated or lengthy. If you are just starting to replace meat in your diet with fish, you will find these recipes become the 'standards' you return to day after day.

In 'Splashing Out' I have concentrated more on fish that are either expensive or harder to track down. Those living in London or near a good fishmonger will be able to find all these varieties with ease, those in other areas may hardly ever come across some of them. The recipes are richer and more elaborate, better suited to a dinner party than a family supper. These dishes tend to use more butter and cream than those in the rest of the book, but since they are reserved for special occasions, your weekly intake will not be high.

I have a great many friends and relations who live in rural areas, where even fresh fish, let alone the more exotic species, are not widely available. Perhaps there is a fishmonger in the nearest town (ten miles away) or a fish van calls round door to door on Fridays, offering even then only the most common varieties: cod, haddock, plaice. 'All Washed Up' is specifically aimed at these readers, written not only with sympathy but with thanks and appreciation for the excellent meals I have eaten in their homes, concocted from pretty run-of-the-mill raw ingredients. Too many cookery books are written by those living in big towns for others who also have easy access to good food shops and big markets.

The Advantages of Fish

Few people realize that fish is one of the most nutritionally near-perfect foods. Unlike meat, which is made up principally of connective tissue protein, fish is mainly muscle tissue protein, which is much more easily digested. White fish are low in all fats, while oily fish like herring and mackerel are low in saturated fats yet high in the unsaturated fatty acids that the body needs, as well as being the richest food sources of vitamins A and D. All fish are low in sodium and good sources of the B complex vitamins as well as of valuable minerals like potassium, iron and phosphorus. A 4 oz (110 g) serving of fish provides half the amount of protein needed by the body each day.

For those watching their weight, white fish like cod or haddock offer as little as 84 calories per 4 oz (110 g) portion, with oily fish containing around 264 calories. This is well below a similar-sized portion of beef (300 calories), pork (368) or lamb (380). Of course, you must add to this the ingredients included in the cooking process, but simply grilled, poached or baked fish is ideal for anyone who cares about their health.

There is not much wastage with fish, since the bones are generally light and can anyway be used to make excellent stocks, and there is also little shrinkage or weight loss during cooking. Since fish requires such a short cooking time it saves on fuel bills, too.

Buying and Choosing Fish

Personally, I believe that the best way to buy fish is from a traditional fishmonger. With a few exceptions, you will be dealing with someone who not only has years of experience and a wide knowledge of the trade, but also a system which is geared to helping the consumer. If you have one in your area you are lucky, because sadly there has been a steady decline in numbers — from nearly 5,000 in the early 1970s to just over 3,000 in Britain today — due primarily to cod wars and raging inflation rather than to anything else. Cultivate your fishmonger well, he (or she — and there are quite a few female ones) will advise you on how to identify the different varieties, on portion size and cooking methods, as well as skinning, filleting and gutting your fish for you — all free of charge.

Recently, supermarkets have begun to expand their fish sales, some even setting up staffed wet fish counters within their larger stores. These now account for 16 per cent of the market. Unfortunately the people who serve you, albeit willing and courteous, often lack detailed experience of the trade or any control over the supermarket's buying policy. However, this is very much a developing area, and with growing demand standards are likely to improve.

Likewise, one effect of high unemployment in the 1980s has been the growth of one-man mobile fish vans selling and delivering door to door, set up with a lump-sum redundancy payment. These vans are certainly convenient, especially for those who can't get to a fishmonger, but again the advice and help available may sometimes be fairly limited.

When choosing whole fish, you should try to ensure that it is as fresh as possible. The eyes should be bright and clear, not dull and sunken. The gills should be scarlet and the body firm, not flabby. If when you press on the skin the dent made by your fingertips does not rapidly disappear, you are justified in speculating on how long it has lain on the slab. Filleted fish should have a glossy gleam to the flesh, which should be a translucent colour and not have dried up round the edges. Frozen fish should be hard frozen and not contain many ice crystals in the pack. If the fish has any white patches or discolouration it has been incorrectly packed and suffered from freezer burn, which ruins its texture.

Should you ever buy a fish which is not fresh, or a shellfish which turns out to be bad, don't take refuge in British reserve — complain! The supermarket or fishmonger where you bought it will be just as concerned as you — their reputation, after all, relies on satisfied customers.

Although there are stringent quality and health controls at wholesale markets, something may slip through the net and your retailer will want to take it up with his supplier if he's been sold a dud. When a fishmonger goes to buy at Billingsgate every morning, for example, he only sees a sample of the consignment of, say, herring that he is buying. The rest is boxed up outside in the chilled lorries which brought it from the port, waiting for the porters to transfer direct to his van. Obviously a good fishmonger buys from wholesale suppliers he can trust, but he will want you to tell him if a fish turns out to be below the standard he paid for.

Stores

Fish is a food which must be eaten at its freshest. Likewise it responds best to being cooked with equally fresh ingredients. Although there are recipes in this book showing you how to make the most of frozen and tinned fish (unfortunately all that is available to many people in this country), if you want to eat fresh fish regularly, you will have to do a small amount of daily shopping.

To keep this task to a minimum, it is a good idea to have a basic supply of those ingredients you use most often in fish cookery always to hand in the kitchen. Then all you have to do is pop into the fishmonger to buy the catch of the day. You will sometimes find that the fish you had planned to eat that night is not available, but if you keep a stock of things like white wine, onions, lemons and fresh herbs at home, you will find you can adapt a recipe or concoct another dish using different fish, without having to rewrite your entire shopping list. So try and fall into the habit of keeping fresh lemons and herbs in the fridge and a reserve of other items in the storecupboard.

These are the basics I use most in cooking fish:

Lemons   The thin-skinned variety contain the most juice. Always have two or three at the bottom of the fridge.

Onions   These keep for quite a while if you select unblemished ones and store them in cool, dark, dry conditions.

Fresh parsley   If you have a garden to grow this in, so much the better. Townies will find, however, that it does not seem to thrive well in window boxes and it is easier bought in large bunches from a market stall or greengrocer. Either store it, stalks down, in a jar of water and chop it as and when needed, or chop the whole lot in one go and keep it in the fridge — in which case watch out it is not too wet or it will go off and smell like old grass cuttings!

Dry breadcrumbs   These can easily be made from a day-old loaf of white or brown bread. Chunks can quickly be reduced to crumbs in a liquidizer or food processor, or more laboriously on a hand grater. Spread the crumbs on a baking tray and dry, but don't brown them, in a low oven. Stored in a tin with a tight-fitting lid, they will keep for months. Ready-made dried white breadcrumbs (with no added colour) are available in fishmongers, and wholemeal ones in good supermarkets. The wholemeal crumbs can be quite large and it is a good idea to whizz them up in your machine to break them down.

White wine   You will use this constantly when cooking fish. It really gives a lift to soups, stocks and sauces and is important for a good court bouillon when poaching. I find it easier to buy a box of fairly cheap white table wine and keep this in the fridge solely (if possible!) for cooking. Opening a bottle merely to use one glass for a sauce is uneconomical.

Bayleaves, peppercorns, parsley stalks   Essential for making good fish stocks and court bouillons. When you have chopped your parsley, wrap the stalks in clingfilm and store in the freezer, for popping directly into the saucepan.

Fresh dill   A herb that goes very well with many fish dishes, this is quite difficult to find, unless you can grow your own. Whenever you see a large bunch on sale, buy it, chop it finely and freeze. This is not as good as fresh dill, but a great improvement on the dried variety.

Oatmeal   You can buy this loose in wholefood shops. When cleaning shellfish like mussels and clams, leave the scrubbed live molluscs in a sink of salty water. Sprinkle about half a mug of fine oatmeal over the surface and leave for a few hours. The shellfish ingest it and expel any sand and mud inside their bodies. Coarse oatmeal is excellent as a coating for fried fish.

Flour   For comments on the use of wholemeal flour, see Béchamels (page 182) and Shortcrust Pastry (page 190).

Preserved Fish

Fish preserved in tins or brine are far removed from the wonderful flavour of fresh fish. However there *are* some good dishes you can make using 'storecupboard' fish. These are the varieties I would recommend keeping a reserve fund of: tinned sardines (in oil rather than tomato sauce); smoked oysters and smoked mussels; tuna; pink salmon; anchovies (apart from the rather salty tinned ones, you can buy fresh anchovies preserved in an oily brine, which taste much closer to the real thing); tinned crabmeat (not dressed crabmeat). It is also worth keeping in the fridge some mussels preserved in brine.

Frozen Fish

Thankfully, we now seem to be emerging from the period when the freezer was god. Most cooked dishes do not benefit from being frozen, fish least of all. Sometimes it is useful to freeze the odd leftover portion of soup for when you are alone, but even then a cooked dish should not be frozen for more than three months maximum.

However, much raw fish is frozen on board the vessel from which it was caught, or at the dockside if caught inshore. Bought in this state it is often of better quality than a tired 'fresh' plaice or whatever, that has been hanging around the supermarket shelf for a few days. Choose your frozen fish with care, find a brand which includes minimal water in the final weight, and stick with it. You will find the freezer can be a useful back-up to your fish cookery, particularly at the beginning of the week when many fresh fish outlets are closed.

Varieties worth keeping in the freezer are coley, cod, haddock, and some of the smoked fish like haddock and kippers. Much shellfish is bought frozen anyway, owing to the dangers of rapid deterioration of fresh shellfish if kept, even under the most stringent conditions, for more than a day. Frozen crabmeat is of a high quality and is sold separately packed into brown and white meat. Frozen scallops are good and often cheaper than fresh ones, and both scampi (langoustine) and crawfish (langouste) tails survive freezing quite well.

Prawns are the most common frozen shellfish — see page 52 for details.

Equipment

All cooks have different eating habits, incomes and kitchens. If you are fairly new to fish cookery, you will soon find there are some recipes you turn to again and again while others, although fun to try, don't suit your individual cooking style or budget. Likewise you will soon realize which particular pieces of kitchen equipment you find indispensable when cooking fish and which, although handy, may not be essential for preparing the sort of dishes you prefer.

These days we are bombarded by advertizing and magazine articles all urging us to buy the latest kitchen gadget. The choice is overwhelming, the quality often variable. Before buying always ask yourself, 'Would I really use this, and is there room for it in my kitchen?' You'd be surprised how much you can improvise, particularly when you're on a limited budget. Some items are worth spending money on, like a good set of kitchen knives or a sturdy chopping board. Others, like colanders and measuring jugs, can be picked up for a few pence at jumble sales.

Only you can know what you need, but here I give a few guidelines to the equipment I find I use most often when cooking fish.

Food processor   After standard fixed equipment like a fridge and sink, this is probably one of the more expensive items in your kitchen. One snag with processors is their tendency to reduce everything to a purée if you turn your back for an instant, so spend a little more and get one with a pulse button for extra control. You can then chop raw ingredients without risking having them end up like babyfood. I find it's not worth using mine to chop the odd onion (by the time I've washed it up afterwards I could have done it by hand), but it is invaluable for grating cheese, making shortcrust pastry and in particular for chopping fish and vegetables to the right consistency for making mousses, pâtés and fish balls. It also liquidizes soups, though not quite as well as a straightforward liquidizer, and makes mayonnaise in no time.

Knives   It is essential to have a few really sharp, good-quality knives. Fish has a delicate flesh — it doesn't want to be mangled by blunt blades. Good knives cost money, but last forever and take hours off your preparation time. In fish cookery you should have a carbon-steel 7-inch (18 cm)* flexible filleting knife, which you can also use for skinning fish fillets. Keep it razor sharp on a knive-sharpener or, better still, a real 'steel', as well as dry or it will rust. Don't even think of using it for levering the lids off tins or anything else that will damage the blade.

Measurements refer to length of blade.

You will also need a 5-inch (13 cm) cook's knife for general use. A stainless steel one is best, since citrus and onion juice stain carbon steel black. Lastly, a large 8-inch (20 cm) chopping knife with a broad blade is useful for chopping fresh herbs, mushrooms and so on at high speed. With your fingertips, hold the pointed end of the blade down on the board and move the knife in an arc, chopping down all the time. Using this professional technique with a large sharp knife, you will quickly have finely chopped parsley, dill or chives to sprinkle on your fish dishes.

Fish slice   This is invaluable for lifting fish steaks and fillets out of a poaching liquid or the frying pan. If you are trying to manoeuvre whole fish like trout or herring after cooking, you will find a long stainless steel spatula is the answer. It also comes in handy when lifting pastry from the board after you have rolled it out.

Slotted spoon   You will use this again and again for skimming the scum from fish stock, testing vegetables when boiling, or removing fish balls from frying pans or saucepans. Always buy stainless steel, both here and when choosing a fish slice, as plastic ones soon melt in hot pans.

Scissors   A good pair of sharp kitchen scissors with pointed ends pays back its expense time and time again. Scissors are much the easiest tool to use to cut the fins off a fish, and also to open its belly for gutting. Hide them in a drawer from the rest of the household, or they will soon disappear.

Sieve   If you have a food processor or liquidizer for puréeing soups, you will use your sieve more as a strainer. A conical strainer, sometimes called a Chinese strainer since it resembles a coolie's hat, is useful as its design means the liquid streams straight through just at the bottom, rather than splashing out all round. Again stainless steel is best.

Measuring jug   This is fairly important for making soups and getting the right proportion for sauces. The 2-pint size with pints, fluid ounces and millilitres marked on is the most versatile.

Grater   Although you can grate cheese and vegetables successfully in a food processor, you will still need a small-toothed hand grater when a recipe calls for grated lemon, lime or orange rind. Whole nutmegs can be shaved against it too.

Pastry brush   A cheap tool for brushing fish while grilling, oiling flan tins or silver foil and glazing pastry with beaten egg. Wash it well after use or it gets rather rancid.

Chopping board   Wooden ones are definitely better and safer than plastic, which may cause the food or your knife blade to slip around. I find a little 6-inch (15 cm) one is handy for cutting lemon wedges, garlic cloves etc., but for most jobs you should choose one that is at least 18 inches (45 cm) square and not too thin. Don't leave it in water or it will warp, but scrub well after use. You may prefer to keep a separate one just for handling raw fish on, as the flavour does tend to permeate the wood after a while.

Saucepans You will need a large pan for making stock, cooking mussels and boiling crabs or lobsters. A small non-stick saucepan is helpful for making smooth sauces. You will also need something to poach whole fish or fillets in. If you are doing this on top of the stove, you can use a clean frying pan or even better, a straight-sided heavy French sauté pan. But for poaching in the oven an ovenproof glass or china oval dish is best — white gratin dishes with flat-lipped ends are pretty enough to bring straight to the table. For poaching larger fish a clean roasting tin is fine.

Fish kettles These are expensive and take up a lot of storage space. Frankly, unless you are going to be cooking a lot of large fish like salmon or sea bass, I wouldn't advise getting one. Instead, if you wrap your salmon in a watertight envelope of oiled silver foil with some white wine and herbs, it can be cooked very successfully on a baking tray in the oven.

THE BARE BONES

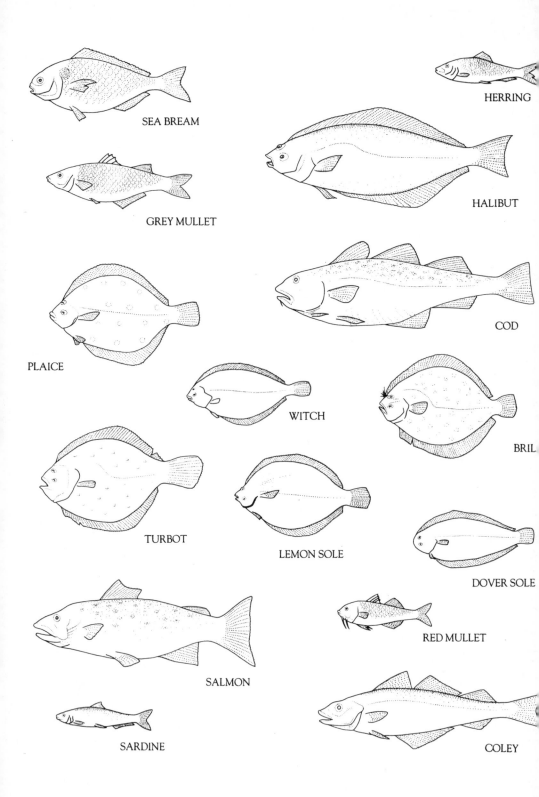

SEA BREAM

HERRING

GREY MULLET

HALIBUT

PLAICE

COD

WITCH

BRILL

TURBOT

LEMON SOLE

DOVER SOLE

SALMON

RED MULLET

SARDINE

COLEY

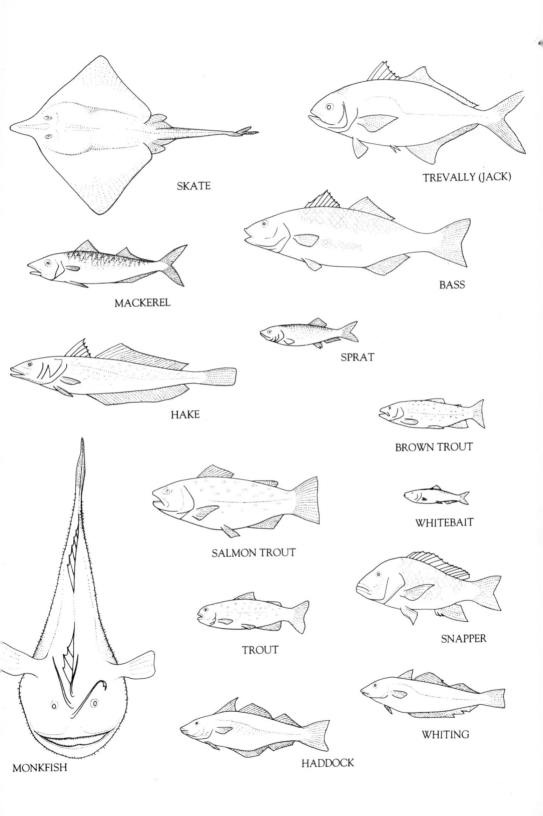

SKATE

TREVALLY (JACK)

MACKEREL

BASS

SPRAT

HAKE

BROWN TROUT

SALMON TROUT

WHITEBAIT

TROUT

SNAPPER

MONKFISH

HADDOCK

WHITING

A to Z of Fish

It should be noted that many fish are available throughout the year, if not fresh from our waters, then imported frozen. The 'seasons' referred to below therefore, as defined by the Sea Fish Industry Authority, are the best months for buying fish when it is both fresh and at a reasonable price.

Bass (Sea Bass)   Season: August-March

The sea bass is a big, long handsome fish which looks beautiful on the fishmonger's slab, its silver-grey scales gleaming. In this way it somewhat resembles a salmon and certainly almost any recipe for salmon can be used for cooking sea bass. Sadly, its price is also on a par with, or even higher than, salmon.

You may well have eaten sea bass in France, where it is called loup de mer (sea wolf) and highly esteemed gastronomically. The flesh is firm but delicate and can be treated gently by poaching it, or sizzled in a spicy Chinese sauce (see recipe), with equal success.

It should be scaled carefully so as not to damage the skin — your fishmonger will do this for you. Allow 12 oz (335 g) of whole fish, uncleaned and with the head on, per person.

Bream (Sea Bream)   Season: June-February

The variety of sea bream available in Britain is also popular on the east coast of the United States, where it is known as porgy. If you can find it, it makes for very good cooking, but it is not widely available and you should not make the mistake of confusing it with a snapper, which it resembles in looks but not in taste.

A sea bream has large scales which need to be removed, and the classic nursery-book shape of a fish — deep body, flattened snout and large fins (which are also sharp and should be cut off before cooking). The flesh is firm and stands up well to tasty sauces.

A sea bream of 1½ lb (670 g) will serve 3 people, but you can find them up to 2½ lb (1.1 kg).

Brill
Season: June-February

This flat fish looks a bit like turbot, but its flesh is not as white or firm. Nonetheless it has a very good flavour which is wasted if it is swamped with too-strong sauces. Brill weigh anything between 1 lb and 5 lb (450 g and 2.25 kg). One of 3 lb (1.35 kg) can be cooked whole by poaching or steaming to serve up to 6 people; larger ones are sold cut into fillets, which should be skinned before being cooked, allowing 6 oz (170 g) a head.

Cod
Season: June-February

One of Britain's most popular fish, cod accounts for around 13 per cent of our annual wet-fish sales. Its abundance and low cost tend to encourage fish snobs to dismiss it as 'ordinary' which is a pity because it has a firm flesh and good taste, so long as it is fresh and cooked with some sensitivity.

Those caught inshore are better quality than deepwater cod, mainly because they have less far to travel to market. You can often tell the difference by the whiter flesh and sheen still visible on the inshore catch — Aberdeen is a particularly good port for this type.

Cod is sold already cut into fillets (allow 6 oz/170 g per portion) or steaks, both equally good. Cod cheeks are excellent but hard to find. You should skin cod before cooking if you have fillets; with a steak it is easier to remove the skin just before serving.

Dried salted cod is popular in Portugal (where it is known as bacalao) and other Mediterranean countries, where it was introduced to cope with the huge demand for fish on Fridays and during Lent. This needs 24–48 hours' soaking in frequent changes of water before cooking.

Smoked cod is sold in fillets and should be cooked before eating. It is nowhere near as good as smoked haddock.

The hard female cod's roe is usually sold smoked in a large, brownish-red, rather off-putting lump. Choose roe that has no artificial dye or preservatives, skin it and soak in water for 30 minutes to remove any saltiness. Smoked cod's roe is the main ingredient of the pâte taramasalata (see recipe), although the original Greek version is made with grey mullet's roe.

Haddock, hake, coley and whiting are all members of the same family as cod, and may be used fairly interchangeably in recipes (although see each fish below for details).

Coley (Coalfish, Saithe)   Season: August-February

This is generally sold as fillets, often frozen. It is even cheaper than cod and at one time was considered by many as fit only for the cat, which is unfair as, although not of a very exciting flavour, coley is excellent for fish pies and soups. Do not be put off by the greyish-brown colour of the raw fish. When cooked it turns perfectly white.

It should be skinned before cooking — allow 6 oz (170 g) per head.

Haddock   Season: May-February

Another staple fish in British cuisine, haddock is as good as cod although it has a rather softer texture. It is usually sold in fillets (allow 6 oz/170 g per portion), but steaks are also available. Fillets should be skinned before cooking.

Smoked haddock is smoked on the bone (as in Finnan Haddock which is the best) or in fillets. With the current public concern about food containing additives and artificial dyes, there is a move away from the bright yellow fillets towards ones of a pale yellow colour, cured and preserved naturally.

Arbroath Smokies are haddock (or sometimes whiting) hot-smoked to a dark brown colour. Although the flesh is already cooked, it is usual to reheat smokies by brushing them with butter and grilling lightly.

Regular smoked haddock should be cooked before being eaten — poaching in milk is a common method.

Hake   Season: June-March

This is less common in Britain than are other members of the cod family, although popular in Portugal and particularly northern Spain, where they cook it in many different delicious ways. You can recognize it on the slab by its long, rather thin shape and grey skin.

Hake is often sold in steaks (allow one per person) but can be found as fillets, which should be skinned before cooking.

Halibut
Season: June-March

An excellent and expensive fish, a whole halibut can be several metres long and weigh a massive amount. For this reason, although it is a flatfish like plaice or sole, the flesh is generally sold as steaks, since the body is so thick. These are often quite large and one weighing 10–12 oz (280–335 g) will feed 2 people. Smaller halibut are filleted — allow about 6 oz (170 g) a portion.

The flesh is quite firm, almost meaty, but tends to be dry if not cooked with care. A smaller variety, known as chicken halibut, is sometimes available and is sold whole. Smoked halibut from Denmark is a real delicacy, but has a high fat content.

Skin steaks before or after cooking, and fillets before.

Herring
Season: May-December

Easily recognizable by its small silver-blue scales, herring is very nutritious, being particularly rich in protein, iodine and vitamins A and D. It is also very cheap, but its numerous fine bones put off many people — you may prefer to serve it filleted or boned whole. Allow 2 small whole herring (less than 6 oz/170 g) per person or 1 large (6–8 oz/ 170–225 g).

The flesh is quite oily, so can be grilled very successfully, and it goes well with sharp sauces.

Good male herring roes, known as milts, are a delicacy lightly fried, but avoid ones that have been frozen in a great block as they tend to be a bit battered and bruised. They are in season around Christmas time.

There are three types of smoked herring: bloaters, buckling and kippers. Bloaters come from East Anglia, particularly Great Yarmouth, where they have been popular for hundreds of years. They are best in the autumn but being ungutted their rather gamey taste doesn't suit everyone. They should be cooked on the day of purchase as they do not keep — fillet, brush with butter and grill.

Buckling are hot-smoked herring with a tough skin that lifts off easily before eating, rather like a smoked trout's. They need no further cooking and are good skinned and served in salads.

Kippers have been cold-smoked and need poaching or grilling before serving. Choose ones that are plump and contain no artificial dye since this, apart from anything else, means the kipper does not keep well. All kippers, however, should be eaten within a few days of purchase.

Herrings are also available pickled and marinated and these are ready to eat.

Mackerel
Available all year, best April-June

These popular, cheap fish, with their distinctive smooth dark-green and black bodies, are widely available and absolutely delicious if really fresh. After a day or so the flesh becomes soggy and tastes unpleasant. The bones are easy to deal with on your plate, so it is not necessary to fillet the fish. The flesh is rich and quite oily, so a sharp sauce like mustard, rhubarb or gooseberry goes well.

Smaller mackerel weighing around 8–11 oz (225–310 g) serve one, but some mackerel are very large and can be divided between 2 people.

Smoked mackerel is good in salads or pâtés and needs no further cooking.

Monkfish (Angler Fish)
Available all year

Legend has it that the reason fishmongers only display the tailpiece of a monkfish is that the rest of the fish is so hideous it would put off the customers. The truth is that the tail is the only bit really worth eating. By all appearances it seems to grow virtually straight out of the (indisputably ugly) head, the 'body' being rather non-existent.

Monkfish deserves a wider following — the flesh is firm and sweet and there is only one central cartilaginous bone to deal with. It is excellent for dishes where texture is important and ideal for kebabs. It is sold skinned — allow 5–6 oz (140–170 g) per person.

Mullet, Grey
Season: September-February

A long silver-grey fish, covered in scales that need to be removed before cooking, the grey mullet is a herbivorous inshore fish. Because it gets its food from the bottom of the sea or estuary, some claim the flesh can taste rather muddy, but personally I've never experienced this. It has a delicate flavour and is well suited to stuffing. It is reasonably priced and becoming more common in fishmongers.

Choose whole ones weighing about 1-1¼ lb (450-550 g). These serve 2 people.

Mullet, Red

Season: May-November

These are becoming increasingly widely available, fresh in the summer and imported frozen in the winter. Both size and prices fluctuate considerably — the larger ones (about 1¼ lb/550 g) serving 2 people give more flesh for your money, but all too often only the real tiddlers are available (although their flavour is just as good). They should not be confused with grey mullet, which is another family and has a totally different taste and appearance.

Red mullet need to be scaled before cooking. Some people like them ungutted (hence their French name, bécasse de mer — sea woodcock). If this turns your stomach by all means clean them, but leave in the dark brown liver which is excellent.

If you can only find small ones (under 7 oz/195 g), serve 2 per person.

Pilchard. See Sardine.

Plaice

Season: May-February

One of Britain's most popular fish, plaice has got itself a bad name through people consistently overcooking it. The fillets of small plaice are often rather thin, so need just the briefest cooking time. Plaice is a suitable substitute for sole if you find the latter too expensive — it has a good taste and easily digestible texture when really fresh.

Whole plaice are easily recognizable by their two differently coloured sides: one pure white, the other (upper side) sandy brown with orange spots. The brightness of the spots is not an indication of freshness, as the old wives' tale claims.

Allow 2 small fillets per person.

Salmon

Season: May-August

The high status of this superb fish is unfortunately matched by its price, though few other fish can equal its flavour. Salmon is often criminally overcooked which leaves the flesh dry — allow 10 minutes to the pound plus 20 minutes, if poaching a whole one. Steaks take 15 minutes in a court bouillon in a preheated oven.

Wild Scotch salmon is the best and therefore most expensive variety, distinguishable from farmed salmon by its more pointed snout (from annually battling upriver), much wider tail and large dorsal fin (in the middle of the back). Farmed salmon often has black spots on the skin and a more rounded snout. Norwegian farmed salmon is reared in coralled-off fjords before being released into the sea. It then returns to the same fjord for spawning, when it is caught — it could be said to be halfway between a true wild and a farmed variety.

Frozen Canadian or Pacific salmon is available throughout the year but is not comparable to our own Scotch, although it is fine for making mousses and pâtés.

Salmon is at its most expensive early in the year, when it may only be caught by rod and line. In the summer, when netting is allowed, the prices drop. The tailpiece is often sold at a lower price because it contains more bone — and because the fish may have been on the slab for a while, having steaks cut off it. The flesh of the tailpiece, however, is very succulent.

Allow 8 oz (225 g) of whole fish, ungutted, per person.

Smoked salmon   Here again, Scotch outstrips the rest of the field. Many fishmongers sell smoked salmon trimmings at a much lower price, which are excellent for pâté. Find a supplier or brand that you like and stick with it, because it can vary considerably. (Some fishmongers smoke their own.) Foreign smoked salmon can sometimes be very salty, or too oily, which is a cruel disappointment after you've emptied your wallet for it.

Salmon Trout (Sea Trout)   Season: April-August

A member of the trout family, this fish is usually called salmon trout because of its pink flesh, although its official name is sea trout. A good one can equal or better a salmon in flavour and certainly beat it for the moistness of its flesh. Being smaller and cheaper than salmon, they are a good choice for a dinner party or family celebration. Cooking methods tend to be similar to salmon, although trout recipes are perfectly acceptable too.

Sardine   Season: March-September

At last whole sardines, imported frozen from the Mediterranean, are being sold in Britain on a widescale basis. They are now reasonably priced and very good, although the many small bones can be a bore to deal with especially if the fish are overcooked, since the bones then break off in the flesh. Sardines are an oily fish and respond well to being cooked with ingredients containing strong flavours — garlic, lemon, fennel, red wine.

They vary in size — allow 8 oz (225 g) per head and scale them before cooking.

Pilchards   These are mature sardines and found mainly on sale in their native West Country. Most of us can only get them in tins. Neither fresh sardines nor pilchards travel well. They should be eaten quickly and scaled before cooking.

Skate   Season: May-February

What you see being sold as skate in British fishmongers are just the wings (modified fins) of this large fish of the shark family. The outer skin is very thick and tough and is generally removed before the fish is put on sale. There are no bones, only a fan of gelatinous cartilage which is easy to remove at the table. The firm flesh is good and quite filling and has a slight ammonia smell which disappears during cooking. Allow 8 oz (225 g) per head.

Snapper   Available all year

Fresh red snappers caught and cooked on the east coast of America and in the Caribbean are excellent. The snappers imported here tend to come from the Mediterranean, frozen, and the flavour has often suffered a bit en route. However the flesh is firm and not bad at all when served with a good sauce. They are quite cheap and more common in areas with a West Indian community. Whole ones weighing 9–10 oz (250–280 g) serve one person. They need scaling before being cooked.

Sole

There is endless confusion about the different types of sole on sale in Britain. In fact the only true sole is the one called after Dover, where the best catches are to be found. The lemon and Torbay (witch) varieties are not in fact sole at all, but can be treated in the same way for culinary purposes.

Personally I prefer to be fairly generous when serving sole and save money elsewhere. I therefore allow one 8–10 oz (225–280 g) sole, filleted, per person or one of 14–16 oz (390–450 g) to serve 2 people. Sole bones make excellent fish stock, so always ask for the trimmings from your fishmonger.

Classic cookery offers dozens of ways of serving sole, but the flavour of a Dover sole is so good it seems a pity to do anything more than skin it

Skate with Orange and Caper Sauce (page 75)

and grill on the bone. If sauces are to be served, they should be light and not swamp the superb taste of this excellent, and expensive, fish.
Dover sole (Season: May-February)   With a firm white flesh and excellent flavour this is easy to distinguish from other flatfish because of its rounded nose and more oval body.
Lemon sole (Season: May-March)   Although inferior to Dover sole, this has a very good flavour and pleasant, if somewhat softer, texture.
Witch (Season: May-February)   This used to be called a Torbay sole, a term that is now illegal. It looks quite like a Dover sole and, although plentiful, it is not that widely available. The flesh, although very white, does not have such a good flavour.

Sprats
Season: November-March

Closely related to the sardine and the herring, sprats are small oily fish about 6 inches (15 cm) long. They are available fresh (in which case they are best simply grilled) and canned. Allow at least 8 oz (225 g) per person for a main course.

Trevally (Jack)
Available all year

A fish not found at all in our waters but imported frozen from New Zealand. Although in looks it resembles a bream or snapper, not being very plump and having the classic picture-book fish shape, its flesh is closer to that of a mackerel in both texture and taste. Not very commonly found, it is worth buying when you see it — for its quite low price it gives good value for money. It weighs anything between 1½ lb and 4 lb (670 g and 1.8 kg), but the large head is quite heavy — a small jack of 1½ lb (670 g) will only serve three.

Trout
Available all year

The trout familiar to most of us are the rainbow variety, whose natural habitat is lakes but who are now being intensively reared on fish farms. The average weight is 10 oz (280 g) which gives one good portion. The flesh is wonderfully moist and has a succulent, slightly sweet taste. Farmed trout offer good value for money and most arrive on your fishmonger's slab within 12 hours of being killed — an enviable record compared to many sea fish. Some farmed trout are rather bland, depending on their diet in their last few weeks, but the industry is beginning to take note of this criticism.
   Brown trout are rarely available commercially, not being suited to farming. They live in faster-running streams and rivers and if you are

Halibut with Pimento Sauce (page 139) and Mussels au Gratin (page 67) ever offered one, don't hesitate to accept the gift — it tastes infinitely superior and should be cooked as simply as possible.

Tuna (Tunny)   Available all year

This is a very large fish, imported fresh in small quantities from the Mediterranean. The flesh is dark pink or even brownish and very meaty. It can be grilled or included in casseroles – the best part is the belly (look out for the word *ventresca* on Italian cans of tuna). Tinned tuna is quite cheap, and good if mixed with salads and sauces, but can be rather dry if served plain. Allow 6-8 oz (170-225 g) per person.

Turbot   Season: April-February, best in summer

This is a superb fish, and much loved by restaurateurs, who charge the earth for a portion. You can easily recognize it when whole: the underside is the usual white as in all flat fish, but the dark-brown upper side is covered in hard little knobs. The flesh is firm but not as dry or meaty as halibut and you can serve it simply baked, poached or grilled. Smaller ones can be cooked whole if you have a large enough pan (try a roasting tin) but it is easier to buy it in steaks or fillets. Allow a 7-8 oz (195-225 g) steak per person, slightly less if filleted, when it should be skinned before cooking.

Whitebait   Available all year

These are very young herring or sprats, caught in large numbers and usually deep-frozen. They are cooked whole, without gutting, the most common method being to fry them and serve with lemon wedges. The best are those up to 2 inches (5 cm) long — bigger ones do not fry up so crisply. Allow 4 oz (110 g) per person for a starter.

Whiting   Available all year

Whiting is a member of the cod family, rarely over 12 inches (30 cm) long and more often about 8 inches (20 cm). Its flesh is delicate verging on bland, but its slightly gelatinous texture makes it very suitable for use in pâtés, terrines and fish balls along with other, stronger-tasting fish. It should be bought very fresh, and it is more economical to buy the larger varieties which the fishmonger can then fillet for you.

Dealing with Fish

Even those already converted to the advantages of eating more fish, both in terms of health and for the speed and infinite variety of cooking methods, are sometimes at a loss when confronted with the raw ingredients. How do you convert that slippery alien *thing* lying on the kitchen table in the paper the fishmonger wrapped it in, into the neatly rolled sole fillets or stuffed mackerel you enjoy eating in restaurants?

Well, the first thing is to throw away the fishmonger's paper, or the moisture from the fish will seep out and the paper will stick to the flesh until you have a rather nasty cardboard-like piece of fish. If you are not going to use the fish immediately, gut and wash it if it is whole, put it on a large plate, covered with clingfilm to keep the aroma from wafting into the butter, and store it in the coldest part of the fridge (the top).

All fishmongers will gut and fillet your fish for you if asked. Some, if they are not too busy, will skin it for you too, or better still show you how this is done. Supermarket fish are usually sold ready-gutted. But should you catch your own, or be in too much of a hurry to wait in the fishmonger's queue for this treatment, here is how it is done.

First identify which of two types your fish belongs to. Imagine it was swimming towards you, head on. Is its body, when seen in cross-section, round/oval or flat? Having categorized your fish, follow the step-by-step guide given here. (My instructions are for right-handed cooks — please reverse where appropriate if you are left-handed.)

Gutting and Cleaning

FLAT FISH   These are nearly always sold already gutted, even at a fishmonger's. If you have to do it yourself, lay the fish, dark skin upwards, on a board next to the sink. Using a sharp knife, make a semi-circular slit just behind the head. Scrape the entrails out of the pocket you have just exposed and wash the fish thoroughly under the cold tap. Cut off the fins with a pair of kitchen scissors and trim the tail. Flat fish do not need scaling.

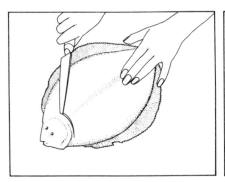 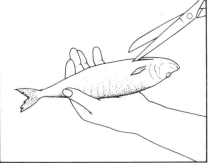

ROUND FISH   Hold the fish firmly in your left hand, belly side up. Using a sharp pair of kitchen scissors, cut the fish open from just under the head to the small anus hole, about half-way along the length of the fish. Scrape out the entrails and wash well under the cold tap, scratching away any dark blood left along the backbone with your thumb.

Some fish (grey and red mullet, sardines and herrings for example), also need scaling. Hold the fish in your left hand and with a small sharp knife scrape the blade in short strokes from tail to head, i.e. against the way the scales lie. You should do this over a newspaper or the kitchen sink and wear an apron as the scales do tend to fly about.

Cut off the fins and gills and trim the tail — some people like to do this into what is called a Vandyke, which is an exaggeration of the tail's natural V shape. (This is named after the fashion for small double-pointed beards set by the seventeenth-century painter Van Dyck.) You can cut off the head as well if you want, just behind the gills.

Filleting

Many recipes call for fish fillets, in other cases filleting is optional and depends on how skilled and/or fussy those sampling your cooking are.

Herrings and sardines, which contain a lot of small bones, are sometimes rather a bore to eat on the bone and children will often tackle with enthusiasm a boned trout which they might otherwise have spurned. When filleting any fish you need a very sharp knife with a flexible blade and it is advisable to keep a separate wooden chopping board solely for handling fish on, as the flavour and aroma tend to permeate it after a while.

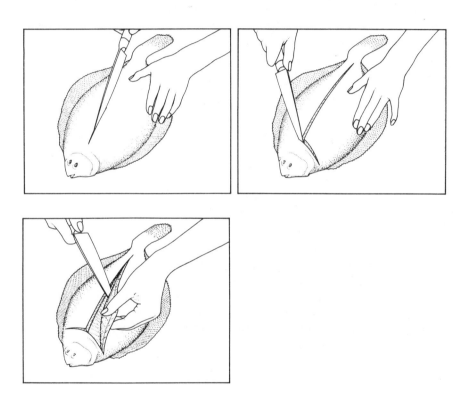

FLAT FISH   Sole and plaice are usually available ready-filleted, but the advantage of buying them whole and then filleting them (or getting the fishmonger to do this for you), is that you can use the bones to make excellent fish stock.

Lay the gutted fish dark-skinned side uppermost and make a cut with the knife in a straight line from head to tail down as far as the backbone. Cut round the head as well. Then, using sharp short strokes and keeping the blade almost flat against the bones, separate one side away, as far as the tail. You should work away from you and from head to tail. Turn the fish round and repeat with the other half, starting from the tail.

Turn the fish over and repeat the whole process on the other side. You will notice that the fillets from the dark-skinned side are the thicker, and you should bear this in mind when serving out the final portions. (Fishmongers often remove the fillets in just two pieces, in which case you can halve them when you get home if they are too large.)

ROUND FISH   Slice the head off the gutted fish and then cut right along the backbone down to the tail. Work the knife down one side of the fish, keeping it close to the bone and working away from you. Use short strokes rather than a sawing motion. When one half is free, detach it from the tail, turn the fish over and repeat on the other side.

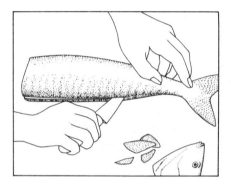

Small round fish like herring, sardines or trout, which you may want to stuff, should be boned in one piece to keep them whole. After cutting off the head, tail and fins, open the fish up as flat as you can, belly side down. Press down with your thumbs along the backbone, which will loosen it, then turn the fish over. You will see that some of the bones have already separated from the flesh. With the end of your knife, starting at the head, continue down the fish, lifting the bone free. A good pair of tweezers is handy for pulling out any bones that get left behind. Reshape and cook as normal.

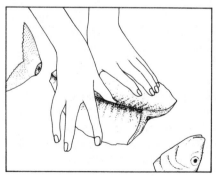
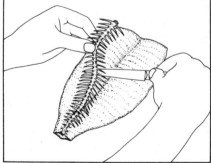

There are times, like when you are serving a whole salmon or salmon trout, when you may want to remove the skin and bone to make it easier to divide into portions. After removing from the court bouillon or silver foil in which it has been cooking, snip through the central bone at the head and tail. Gently scrape off the skin (but work quite fast or it will go cold) and then split the fish from head to tail down as far as the backbone. Lift this carefully out, push the two top fillets together again and serve.

For dressing a whole fish for a cold buffet, see recipe for Cold Salmon Trout.

Skinning

FILLETS   Uncooked fish fillets like sole, plaice or haddock often arrive with skin still on one side, which should be removed before cooking. Lay the fillet, skin side down and tail end towards you, on a board. Sprinkle a little salt over the tail to stop it slipping when you grip it. Hold the tail down firmly with your left fingertips and make a small cut through the flesh just above the tail with a sharp flexible filleting knife. Keeping the knife between the skin and the flesh and at a slight angle, saw gently back and forth, pushing the fillet away from you as it separates from the skin. Continue until you reach the other end. As you get more practised, you will be able to hold the knife flatter and saw less. The important thing is to have a really sharp knife with a flexible blade.

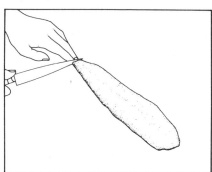 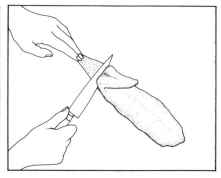

WHOLE FLAT FISH   If you are going to cook a flat fish whole and yet wish to skin it first, lay it on a board dark side uppermost and salt the tail as above. Holding the tail down, make the same cut just above it and with your fingers, work the skin loose from the tail and round the first part of the two edges. Then salt your right hand, grasp this flap of skin and in one movement rip it off. Repeat on the other side if desired.

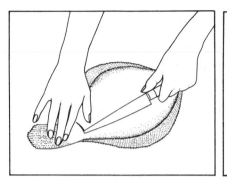 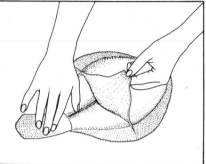

WHOLE ROUND FISH   The skin of these is more closely bonded to the flesh when raw than in flat fish and it is much quicker to scrape the skin off when the fish has been cooked. Turn it over gently and repeat on the other side.

Cooking Fish

POACHING   Suitable for fillets, whole fish or steaks. Place the fish in a shallow pan or saucepan on top of the stove. Heat the court bouillon or milk and pour it round the fish (or alternatively heat the liquid and lower the fish into it, depending on size). Return to poaching temperature, which is just below simmering point, and cover. Never boil fish.

Whole fish	8–10 minutes per 1 lb (450 g)
Fillets	7–9 minutes
Steaks	8–10 minutes

POACHING OR BAKING IN LIQUID IN THE OVEN   Some people do this at Gas 4/350°F/180°C, but I prefer Gas 5/375°F/190°C, which speeds it up a little without damaging the delicate fish.

Whole fish	8 minutes per lb (450 g) + 10–15 minutes
Fillets and steaks	10–15 minutes

STEAMING   Suitable for fillets and thin steaks. Put the fish in a perforated steamer or on a heatproof plate over a saucepan of simmering water. Season and cover tightly.

Fillets	10 minutes
Steaks	15 minutes

GRILLING   Non-oily fish should be brushed with butter or oil to prevent any drying-out. Heating the grill first, with the empty pan under it, helps prevent the fish from sticking while grilling. Plump fish like mackerel can have slashes made in their sides to speed up cooking.

Whole small fish	5–8 minutes each side
Steaks and thick fillets	4–5 minutes each side
Thin fillets	5 minutes (do not turn)

SHALLOW FRYING   Especially good for small whole fish like trout. A mixture of oil and butter prevents the butter burning.

Whole fish	6–8 minutes each side
Steaks and thick fillets	5–6 minutes each side
Thin fillets	4 minutes (do not turn)

DEEP FRYING   This method absorbs a fair quantity of the oil, which should be vegetable or sunflower. Suitable for when a crisp coating is required for breadcrumbed fish. Heat the oil to 350–390°F (180–195°C) before adding the fish.

Whitebait	2–3 minutes
Other fillets or fishcakes	6–12 minutes (+ 4 minutes if frozen)

FOIL BAKING   A good way to cook stuffed or unstuffed whole fish without losing moisture. Set the oven to Gas 6/400°F/200°C.

Small whole fish	15–20 minutes
Steaks and thick fillets	10–15 minutes
Large whole fish (e.g. salmon)	15 minutes per lb (450 g) at Gas 4/350°F/180°C

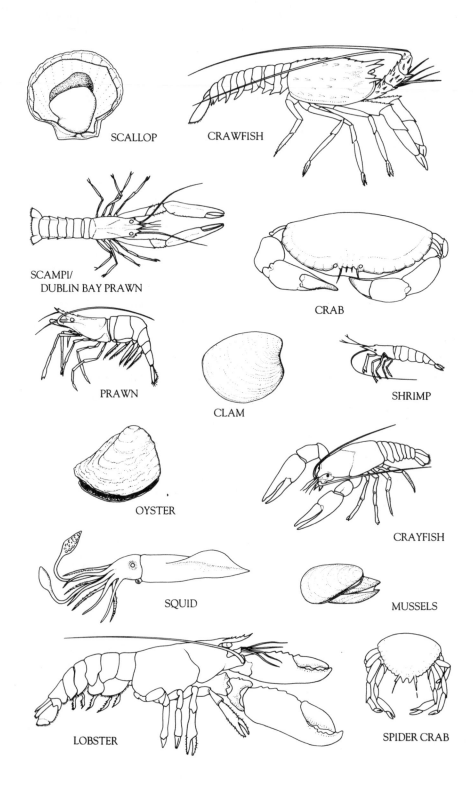

SCALLOP

CRAWFISH

SCAMPI/
DUBLIN BAY PRAWN

CRAB

PRAWN

CLAM

SHRIMP

OYSTER

CRAYFISH

SQUID

MUSSELS

LOBSTER

SPIDER CRAB

A to Z of Shellfish
and How to Deal with Them

Clams
Available all year, best in autumn

Hard-shelled, or round, clams with a shell-width of about 3 inches
(8 cm) are not that well known in Britain but they are worth looking out
for. Sold live in the shell they can be steamed open in the same way as
mussels, but should first be soaked for a few hours in water to which a
couple of spoonfuls of fine oatmeal have been added. Clams are very
sandy and this helps expel most of the dirt. The shells should then be
thoroughly scrubbed, before cooking like a mussel (see below) — this
will take about 10 minutes. Any that remain shut after cooking must be
discarded.

Sometimes you can find small clams with white triangular shells,
known in Italy as vongole, which are excellent cooked in a sauce with
rice or pasta, or poached and included in a salad.

Crab
Available all year, best May-October

The common crab, the large smooth-shelled variety available from
British fishmongers, can weigh between 1 lb and 4 lbs (450 g and
1.8 kg), the most usual being about 1½–2 lb (670–900 g) which will yield
30–40 per cent of its body weight in meat. Choose one that is heavy for
its size (when you pick it up, it is slightly heavier than your eye would
expect it to be). Shake it slightly: you should not hear any water sloshing
around inside. If buying one ready-boiled, make sure the claws are still
firmly attached — flabby joints indicate a certain age.

The white meat, considered the more delicate, is in the claws and central body and the brown, which is creamy and stronger-tasting, in the main shell. For this reason cock (male) crabs are more sought-after than hen (female), as their claws are much bigger. You can recognize a female crab, apart from its smaller claws, by its much bigger 'apron' — the triangular flap on the underside.

Crabmeat is also sold frozen in 1 lb (450 g) packs of either all white meat, or half-half (which is cheaper) — see section on Frozen Fish in Stores. Do not confuse frozen crabmeat with 'crab sticks'. These are cheap, but made (mostly in Japan) entirely from Alaskan coley. They have never been near a crab, although some people find the added taste similar and like them — personally I avoid them at all costs. Ready-dressed crab may also contain bulking-out material like breadcrumbs, so be aware of this when comparing prices.

Cooks pressed for time will opt for frozen crabmeat, but that does rule out attractive dishes served in the shell like dressed devilled crab, as well as really good crab soup using stock made from the shell (see recipes). Extracting the meat yourself takes about 15–25 minutes, depending on the size and your thoroughness.

Spider Crab   This should be as widely available as the common crab, since it is caught off the English coast. But virtually the entire catch is exported to France, where it is rightly considered a delicacy. However, if you live near a port which lands spider crab, like Newhaven, you can sometimes buy it direct on the quay.

The spider crab does not have the large claws of the common variety, and the arrangement of its thin legs resembles that of a spider, hence the name. It is consequently less time-consuming to extract its meat, but obviously it contains less white.

Cooking a Crab

Buying a live crab is preferable to a ready-boiled one as it ensures freshness. One way of killing them recommended by an animal welfare group is to pierce them in two different spots with an awl, but the angle this must be held at and the exact spots to stab are so precise it is not easily achieved by the common cook. Another researcher suggests electrocution — again hardly practical, or indeed safe. Others recommend putting the crab in cold salted water and bringing to the boil as the most humane method (it supposedly loses consciousness and feels no pain). However, this method can lead to the crab's throwing off its claws during cooking, which spoils the taste.

The RSPCA has recently examined the whole issue of killing crustaceans and points out that since they cast off shells and claws with a gay abandon which mammals would hardly adopt to shed limbs, there is some doubt as to whether crustaceans can feel pain at all. The RSPCA gives them the benefit of this doubt and suggests avoiding eating them altogether. Fishermen and cooks with harder hearts throw them into boiling water and put the lid on. For crabs you should allow 15 minutes to the pound (450 g) and cool them in the liquid.

Extracting the Meat

Use a small skewer, large clean hairgrip or an all-metal teaspoon and do it over newspaper, with a large bowl for the cleaned shell and a smaller one for the meat.

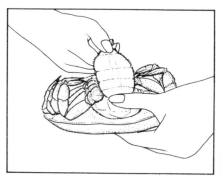 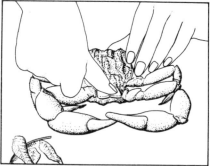

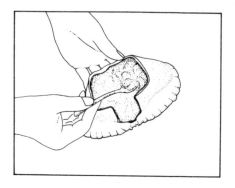

Once cool, pull off the triangular flap underneath and with it the whole central undershell. This should also bring out the intestine and stomach which must be thrown away. You should also discard the 'dead man's fingers' — flat fronds which in spite of their unattractive name are merely tough and inedible, not poisonous! Press down on the small mouth part to remove — it should snap off. Cut the central white body shell into four and pick out the meat.

Twist off the large claws and crack them gently with nutcrackers. Extract the white meat with your skewer — poke around well, because there is quite a lot in there. Pull off the thin legs and do likewise, although in small crabs the last joint of the leg is hardly worth bothering with, it contains so little meat.

Scoop out the brown creamy meat from the large shell. Depending on the dish you are going to make, you may need to keep the two colours separate. Unless you are making dressed crab, return all the bits of shell to the cooking liquid, add a bouquet garni, a few slices of onion and a small glass of dry white wine. Simmer for 15–20 minutes for a really tasty stock.

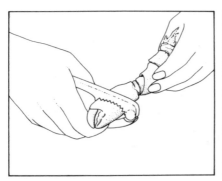 

Crawfish. See Lobster.

Crayfish

Known as écrevisse in France, where these small freshwater shellfish are very popular, this is often mistakenly confused with crawfish. Crayfish look somewhat like a miniature Dublin Bay prawn without the long front claws. The shell is grey-green to black when raw, changing to pink when cooked. They are rarely to be seen on sale in Britain.

Dublin Bay Prawn. See Scampi.

Lobster

Available all year, best April-September

Lobsters are usually sold cooked in Britain, which is fine for any cold dish calling for already-cooked lobster meat. For hot lobster dishes, however, you need to start with a live lobster, which you should be able to order from your fishmonger. A live lobster is dark blue in colour, turning bright orange-red when cooked.

The flesh of a lobster, once extracted from the body and the large claws, is firm and very good, although the price is now so high that many question whether it is not overvalued. However, normal appetites find that half a 1½ lb (670 g) lobster is quite sufficient and for special occasions lobster, like champagne, does add a certain something.

The male is smaller than the female with a narrower tail which is flatter at the sides, but it has larger claws. The flesh of the female is slightly more tender and the body often contains the tiny eggs, known as coral, which are excellent used in sauces.

Often a catch of live lobster not sold after a morning at the wholesale market will be boiled on the spot and sold off cheaply in your fishmonger's — these are a good buy. If you are choosing a ready-cooked lobster, pick it up first. The tail should be tightly curled under the body. If it hangs down and the body shell gives somewhat (what the trade refers to as the 'oil-can' effect), the flesh will be spongy and not worth buying. Most lobsters on sale in Britain weigh 1–2 lb (450–900 g), the best being around 1½ lb (670 g).

Crawfish   The French for lobster is homard, not langouste as many people think, which is in fact crawfish (spiny or rock lobster). The crawfish, which is a brownish colour when uncooked, does not possess the huge front claws of a lobster, but the meat from its tail can be used as a substitute in lobster recipes. Frozen crawfish tails are fairly widely available, not comparable to fresh lobster meat of course, but very acceptable if you choose a European variety.

(For Norway Lobster, see Scampi.)

To Cook

Most fishmongers sell lobster ready-boiled — check that yours does this on the premises for guaranteed freshness. However, should you buy one live, the best method of killing it is to plunge it into boiling water. The popular theory that you can kill it by plunging a knife into the cross-mark where the head joins the body section is doubtful. Lobsters are not vertebrates and therefore this method, which would kill most creatures by severing the spinal cord, does not really apply here. Reassure your squeamishness by bearing in mind that it has no real brain either, only a long nerve cord.

In a large pan bring some salted water to the boil, making sure there is enough to cover the lobster completely. Grip it round the body (the claws should be held together by a strong elastic band, if it has come from a fishmonger), and drop it into the water. Cover with a lid and cook for 20 minutes for one weighing 1 lb (450 g), 30 minutes if weighing 1½ lb (670 g). Those over this weight are liable to contain rather tough meat. Any sound you hear is the air being expelled from underneath the shell due to the change in temperature — lobsters have no vocal chords and cannot 'scream' as popular myth would have it.

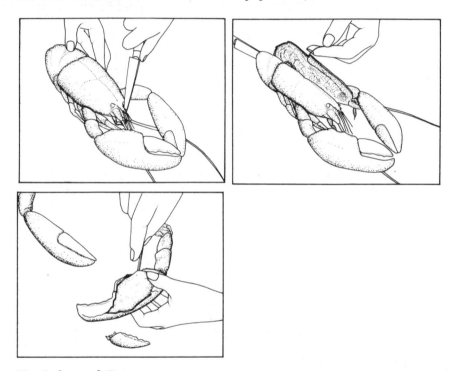

To Split and Dress

Put the cooked lobster on a large board, back uppermost. Using a pair of strong kitchen scissors, poultry shears or a small strong knife, cut from between the eyes right along the large head, down the middle of the back to the end of the tail. Insert the blade of a sharp knife into the slit you have made and cut right through until you have 2 halves. Open these out and remove the dark green-black thread, which is the intestine, and discard it. Also throw away the small semi-transparent sac, resembling a small plastic bag, in the head. This is the stomach and may contain weed. (Do not take out the soft brownish meat around the intestine, this is the liver and has a good flavour.) Unlike a crab, that is all you have to remove.

Twist off the two large claws at the base, being careful not to pull any meat out of the main body of the lobster. Wrap these in a clean tea towel and hit them with a rolling pin to crack them. Remove the claw meat, making sure you separate it from the cartilaginous bone in the centre. Try and keep the chunks of meat as large as possible and put these in a bowl.

Using the scissors again, snip off the small feeler claws, leaving the top joint attached to the body. Snip along one side of each claw and gently open them up to extract the meat without damaging the appearance of the claw, which you can use for decoration later. Discard the hairy claw nearest the head.

Gently lift out the tail meat with the tip of your knife. Slice it diagonally into scollops. Loosen the meat in the main shell with the metal handle of a teaspoon and pull it out of the claw joints with a skewer. This is just to make it easier to eat at the table. Replace the claw meat from the bowl neatly into the lobster body. Arrange the tail scollops, rounded side up, in the opposite tail-half to the one you extracted them from. You will find they fit very neatly and this way the attractive pink side is uppermost. Wipe round the edge of the shell with a damp cloth.

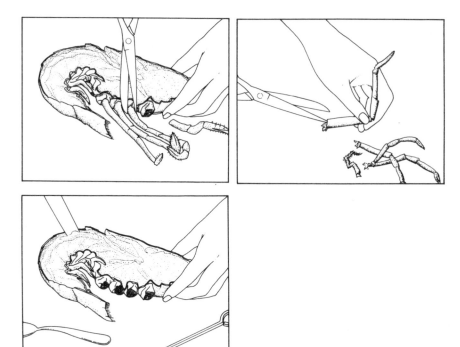

Mussels
Season: September-March

Mussels are cheap shellfish which lend themselves to more dishes than is generally realized. Those gathered round the British shores, from places like Devon and East Anglia, are traditionally sold by the quart (2 pints) although most fishmongers (as opposed to shellfish stalls) now sell them by the pound, which makes it easier to compare them in price to French and Dutch mussels, imported from mussel farms and sold by the kilo. Imported mussels are usually more expensive for their weight, but being smaller have a more delicate flavour. They are also cleaner and require less scrubbing.

Mussels' ideal habitat is round a harbour mouth, clinging to breakwaters and jetty supports, although farmed ones are located in less inhabited estuaries. To offset the associated danger of pollution, some suppliers leave them in purifying tanks for 48 hours before bringing them to the marketplace. They are also regularly analysed and checked at markets like Billingsgate (as are all fish and shellfish) for harmful bacteria. If you eat mussels prepared at home, it is extremely rare to encounter a bad one, so long as you follow these rules:

– Buy from a reputable fishmonger who gets a daily supply.

– On getting home, throw out any that remain open when tapped on the side of the sink. They are dead and may well be off. Discard any that have a broken shell.

– Be equally suspicious of those that float or are unnaturally heavy — the latter may be choc-a-bloc with mud and the former dead.

– After cooking, throw out any which have not opened.

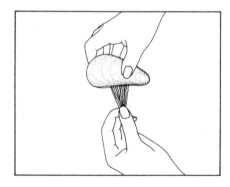

To Clean

It is a good idea, when you first get home, to put your mussels in a sink of cold salted water with 2 or 3 tablespoons of fine oatmeal, or even dried milk. By ingesting this they expel sand and dirt already in the body, and plump up a little. Leave them in this solution for only a couple of hours.

After this soaking, scrub the mussels well at the sink, using a stiff nailbrush. Pull off the hairy beard* which sticks out from between the shells; cut off those that are obstinate with nail scissors. Put the cleaned mussels in a colander and rinse really well under cold running water. They are now ready for cooking.

To Cook

You need a large saucepan containing a very little water, wine and herbs (see individual recipes). Put in the cleaned mussels, cover, bring to the boil over a high heat and cook for just 4–5 minutes at the most, shaking the pan occasionally. All too often in restaurants one is served mussels that are overcooked, where the flesh has become rubbery and wrinkled. Lift the cooked mussels out with a large slotted spoon (discarding any that remain closed).

Oysters   Available imported all year, native September-April

Oysters are one of the most expensive seafoods and nowadays always associated with luxury, although in earlier times they were widely available and eaten by the poor. Native British oysters are considered by many to be the best in the world and are traditionally eaten raw. Different breeds include Whitstable, Helford, and Colchester after their habitats, and grading is done in sizes 1–4, with size 1 being the largest and most expensive. It is still possible to gather your own on more remote coasts like the Scottish Highlands but, as with mussels, make doubly sure that there is no local source of pollution.

Over the past few years the disease bonamia has swept our native oyster beds, killing whole areas and moving from bed to bed, so native oysters are at the time of writing becoming scarce and even more expensive. Since the parasite can live in a fallow oyster bed for three years or so, and then sweep through new stock, hopes of a rapid return to normal for native breeders remain low. Imported oysters, known variously as Portugese, Pacific or Fin de Claire, which are available out

---

*There is some confusion over the term 'beard'. Some recipe books use it to denote the hairy weed-growth I have described above, which is the term employed in this book. Others describe the thin separate band of flesh around the edge of half the mussel (only visible after the shell has opened) as the beard and instruct you to remove it. This is time-consuming and unnecessary, it tastes no different from the rest and pulling it off often leads to the mussel's falling apart, especially in the larger varieties.

of our oyster season anyway, look poised for a takeover. These have a more irregular pear-shaped shell — they are fine for cooking but not a patch on native British ones for eating raw.

All oysters should be eaten absolutely fresh and only opened at the very last minute. To do this, wrap a tea towel round your left hand (if you are right-handed) and, holding the oyster flat-side up in your left palm, slip the point of an oyster knife or other sharp-ended, short, strong knife between the two shells. With a sharp jerk of the knife open the oyster. Detach it from its shell and then return to one shell for serving on a bed of ice.

Oyster purists renounce all strong-tasting accompaniments like Tabasco or Worcestershire sauce, swallowing them whole with just a squeeze of lemon. Those who are less enthusiastic may prefer them cooked, wrapped in bacon (Angels on Horseback) or stuffed (see recipes). You either love 'em or hate 'em, but everybody should try them at least once. Allow 6 per head for a first course.

Prawns Available frozen all year, fresh February-October

Whole prawns are 2½ inches (6 cm) long and when uncooked have a greyish shell, but in Britain they are almost invariably sold ready-boiled in which case their shell has turned the familiar bright pink and curled up. They are also sold peeled, both fresh and frozen, the former being infinitely preferable.

The quality and packaging standards of frozen peeled prawns is now becoming something of a scandal. Although frozen ones appear much cheaper than fresh, up to 30 per cent of the packaged weight can consist of ice, a recent London survey found. Often the taste is disappointing and needs to be jazzed up with strong sauces or spices. Norwegian or Scottish frozen prawns are of a higher quality than Indian ones, which are cheaper but fit only (in my opinion) for a curry so fiery that other tastes become irrelevant. On the other hand a packet of prawns in the freezer is a useful standby to use in sauces or other composite dishes. They, or any other shellfish, should not be stored in a domestic freezer for more than 2 months.

Mediterranean Prawn (Crevette) This is a giant version of the familiar prawn, with a clearly segmented body. It is about 4–5 inches (10–13 cm) long, usually frozen and very expensive — restaurants can charge £1 or more *per creature*. They do, however, create a tremendous visual effect on a large seafood platter, even if you only use a few. It is usual, if serving them plain with the garlic mayonnaise aioli (which is delicious if rather antisocial), to remove the body shell but keep the head on so the prawn can easily be dipped in the sauce.

To Peel a Cooked Prawn

This method applies equally to shrimps, Dublin Bay prawns and Mediterranean prawns, though obviously the smaller the creature the more fiddly it becomes. Hold the prawn in your fingertips in the middle of its back. Pull off the head and tail, then pull the legs downwards. As they come off, the shell will half detach and you should be able to pick it off fairly easily. Quite a good stock can be made with the discarded shells, heads, etc.

Scallops
Season: September-March

These familiar ribbed bivalves are almost always sold by fishmongers ready-opened with the edible part, the muscle, left attached to the flat half-shell. The flesh should be firm and white. However you can always ask for the rounded shell to be included when you buy scallops, as this is a useful and attractive 'dish' on which to serve individual cooked portions. Should you ever need to open them yourself, follow the same method as for oysters.

The curved pink coral is eaten as well, but it is usual to cut off and throw away the thin wavy part round the edge, unless you want to include it in a shellfish soup. Cut the scallop off its shell in one piece with a sharp knife or scissors and wash well. Scrub the rounded shell with a nail brush if you are using it. Scallops can be sliced into 2 or 3 horizontally, depending on thickness.

Scallops (sometimes called scollops) are also available frozen off the shell, as are queens, which are a smaller variety.

Scampi (Dublin Bay Prawn, Norway Lobster)
Available frozen all year, fresh April-November

This is the largest type of British prawn and easily recognizable when whole by its very long thin front claws. The pale pink shell goes orange when cooked, but you can occasionally find them raw. They come to Billingsgate fresh from Scotland — any not sold that day are cooked and just the tails sold, a process which of course further increases the price. Frozen scampi tails are sold in good fishmongers and also in Chinese supermarkets (where you can often find other frozen shellfish, imported from the Far East and much cheaper than British varieties, but of variable quality).

If you ever go to the Adriatic or Eastern Mediterranean and can try local scampi don't hesitate, since it is generally much better than the kind available in Britain.

Shrimps Season: February-October

It should be noted that in America all prawns are referred to as shrimp, which is confusing for British people but quite logical since they are all related to the same family. Efforts are being made here by Government bodies and the fishery industries to get us to adopt this transatlantic custom, without much success so far. (I have used the familiar terms of everyday shop-language for this book, rather than the correct species names.)

In Britain what we call a shrimp is a very small crustacean, about 1–1½ inches (2.5–4 cm) long with a brownish shell when cooked. (The pink ones available are not as good.) They are fiddly to peel and many people are happy to eat them with the thin shells still on. Peeled they make a good shrimp sauce (see recipe) or can be potted with butter, but frozen peeled shrimps, usually imported from the Far East, are virtually tasteless.

Both unpeeled shrimps and unpeeled prawns, when sold from a shellfish stall rather than in a fishmonger's or supermarket, are measured by pints and half-pints. A pint is very roughly equal to 12 oz (335 g) of peeled and 10 oz (280 g) unpeeled shrimps or prawns.

Squid Season: May-October

Technically squid are cephlapods, the same family as octopus and cuttlefish. However for many people they create the same problems as shellfish — i.e. how to prepare them ready for cooking — which is why I have included them in this section.

Some squid are very large — the largest within recent memory sold at Billingsgate weighed in at 14 stone or so, with tentacles as thick as a man's arm. Generally the ones on sale in Britain have a body length (not including tentacles) of between 3 and 10 inches (7–25 cm), all equally good. They are usually imported frozen, but stand up to it well.

Many people are very put off by the appearance of squid and further discouraged by not knowing how to deal with them. This is a pity because they are delicious, with a firm texture and good taste that adapts well to dozens of recipes.

To Prepare for Cooking

Put the squid in a bowl by the sink and prepare them one by one. First, pull off the head — most of the intestine should come out of the tubular body with it. Cut off the tentacles where they join the head and remove the lacy purple skin if they are large (it may not come off small tentacles very easily, in which case leave it). Discard the head.

 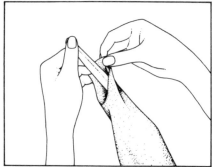

Put your finger down inside the body and pull out the transparent cartilage, which you should throw away. Wash the inside of the body well until very clean and rub off the purple skin with your thumb under the tap. You can either slice the body and chop the tentacles, or leave them whole, depending on the recipe.

The silver thread which usually comes out when you pull off the head is the ink sac. If you break this, everything is rapidly covered with black ink — messy, but you can see why this is an effective defence for the squid when attacked in the sea. This ink is perfectly edible, and should you wish to use it in a recipe, put the sacs into a small bowl to keep them intact till ready to use.

Squid should be cooked either for a very short time (until they turn white) or for an hour or more. Anything in between and they will be rather tough and rubbery, which is sadly how many people first encounter squid in bad restaurants.

SWIMMING ALONG

Soups and Starters

Cream of Fish Soup

This is a satisfying soup that brings out the delicate flavour of whiting, which is one of the cheapest varieties of fish on the market. Buy large ones to prevent wastage and ask your fishmonger to fillet them. Make sure you take the bones home too, for they make an excellent stock. I prefer not to liquidize this soup, but instead to mash the cooked fish well with a fork.

Serves 4

12 oz (335 g) whiting weighed after filleting
1¼ pints (600 ml) fish stock
bayleaf
black peppercorns
slice lemon

¼ pint (150 ml) milk
2½ fl.oz (75 ml) single cream
1 oz (30 g) butter
1 oz (30 g) white flour
seasoning
1–2 tbsp fresh chopped parsley

Either make the fish stock (see page 180) using the whiting bones plus any others you can get from the fishmonger, or use some stock already in your freezer. Skin the whiting fillets and place them in a medium-sized saucepan. Pour about ½ pint (300 ml) of the fish stock over the whiting and add a bayleaf, some crushed black peppercorns and a slice of lemon. Bring to just below a simmer and poach for 10 minutes.

Strain the liquid the fish has cooked in back into the rest of the stock. Mash the fish very well with a fork. Melt the butter in a saucepan, make a roux with the flour and stir in the fish stock to make a smooth consistency. Simmer covered for 10 minutes, add the fish and milk and simmer, uncovered, another 5 minutes.

Test for seasoning, stir in the cream, heat through and serve sprinkled with the chopped parsley.

Coley and Cucumber Chowder

A quick and easy fish soup, with the sharper taste of natural yoghurt in place of a conventional stock. Whiting fillets may also be used.

Serves 4

1 lb (450 g) coley fillets
½ cucumber
7½ fl.oz (225 ml) milk
2 level tbsp cornflour

2 small tubs (total 300 g) natural
  yoghurt
2 tbsp lemon juice
dash anchovy essence
black pepper

Skin the fish fillets and cut them into small dice. Peel the cucumber and chop it finely. Pour the milk into a saucepan and add the cucumber, bring to just under the boil and simmer gently for 10 minutes. Dissolve the cornflour in a little water and add it to the pan with the other ingredients. Heat until nearly boiling and simmer, stirring often, for a further 5–10 minutes until the soup is thick and creamy. The cornflour, apart from thickening the soup, also prevents the yoghurt curdling.

Serve with crusty French bread.

Mussel and Vegetable Broth

This brightly coloured broth is my shellfish variation of those vegetable-based soups found in Italy and Spain like minestrone and menestra, which include a little bit of everything and are filling enough for a light lunch with lots of bread and a salad. To make a real meal of it, add a couple of tablespoons of peeled prawns and a handful of small pasta shapes for the last 10 minutes' cooking. It does take a little while to prepare, but everything up to adding the mussels just before serving can be done in advance.

Serves 4

To cook the mussels
1 quart or 2 lb (900 g) mussels
¼ pint (150 ml) dry white wine
¼ pint (150 ml) water
bayleaf
black peppercorns
parsley stalks

Soup
1 medium leek

2 oz (55 g) button mushrooms
½ medium onion
1 large carrot
1 oz (30 g) butter
1 clove garlic
1 large tbsp wholemeal flour
1½ pints (850 ml) fish stock
8 oz (225 g) tin tomatoes
seasoning
fresh chopped parsley

Scrub the mussels well, discarding any that remain open when tapped. Put them in a large saucepan with the wine and water, the bayleaf, parsley stalks and crushed black peppercorns. Bring quickly to the boil and simmer, covered, for 5 minutes until the shells have opened. Strain the liquid through a sieve into a bowl to catch the mussels, then strain it again through a double piece of muslin into a jug to catch any fine sand and grit. Leave the stock to one side to settle and, using a teaspoon, remove the mussels from their shells, discarding any that have not opened. Put them in a small bowl and set on one side.

Peel the carrot, quarter it lengthways and then slice it thinly across. Do the same with the leek, washing it well afterwards in a sieve to remove any grit. Chop the onion and slice the mushrooms finely. Melt the butter in a saucepan and sweat the sliced vegetables, except the mushrooms, with the crushed garlic for 10 minutes, over a very gentle heat.

Stir in the flour and the tomatoes, crushing the latter thoroughly with a potato masher, and then pour on the fish stock, stirring well to blend in the flour. Add the mussel stock very carefully so as not to disturb the sediment at the bottom. (You will find about a teaspoon of this left, which has managed to get through even the muslin.) Mussel stock is not a very attractive colour, but the tomatoes will camouflage this, and it does taste strongly of mussels, so don't omit it.

Bring to the boil, add the mushrooms and simmer for 10 minutes (putting in the prawns and pasta at this stage if you are including them). Taste for seasoning, add the mussels, heat through and serve sprinkled with the chopped parsley.

Cream of Mussel Soup

The saffron used in this recipe gives the soup a delicate pale yellow colour. The shelled mussels are added whole and you can serve it either as a light broth or thicken it slightly to give a creamier version. Cheap enough to serve as an everyday dish, it is equally good as the opening to a dinner party.

Serves 4

To cook the mussels
1 quart or 2 lb (900 g) mussels, preferably small ones
¾ pint (425 ml) water
1 glass dry white wine
¼ medium onion (sliced)
bayleaf
parsley stalks
black peppercorns

Soup
¼ medium onion
1 oz (30 g) butter
3 sticks celery
1 medium leek
1 clove garlic
pinch saffron
approx. 1 pint (550 ml) milk
3–4 tbsp single cream
1 tbsp white flour (optional)

Scrub the mussels thoroughly, discarding any that remain open when tapped. Put them in a large saucepan with the water, white wine, and other ingredients for cooking the mussels. Cover, bring quickly to the boil and simmer until the shells open, about 5 minutes. Remove them from the pan, discard any that remain closed, and using a teaspoon remove the orange flesh into a bowl. Cover and set to one side. Strain the cooking liquor through a double piece of muslin into a measuring jug.

Finely chop the celery, leek and other onion quarter, rinsing the leek under cold running water to get rid of any grit. Reserve some pale green leek shreds for a final garnish. Melt the butter in a medium saucepan and sweat the vegetables for 10 minutes with the crushed garlic. Add the saffron and the mussel stock, made up to 2 pints (1.1 litre) with milk. If you want a slightly thicker soup, you should stir a tablespoon of flour into the sweated vegetables before blending in the stock and milk. Cover, bring to the boil and simmer gently for 15 minutes.

Liquidize, add the mussels and cream and reheat. Serve sprinkled with the leek shreds for garnish, after blanching them in boiling water to soften.

Taramasalata (Smoked Cod's Roe Pâté)

Homemade taramasalata has a delicate flavour and pale colour that is far removed from the oversalted version offered in most delicatessens and Greek restaurants, which is artificially coloured with food dye to a hideous bright pink. The quantities here make 12 oz (335 g) of finished pâté which works out cheaper than the bought version, as well as being utterly delicious. You will need a food processor or liquidizer, unless you are very patient and prepared to pound it all in a pestle and mortar.

Serves 6 or more

4 oz (110 g) smoked cod's roe	black pepper
1 thick slice white bread	¼ pint (150 ml) olive and sunflower
2 tbsp milk	oil mixed
¼ medium onion	juice of ½ lemon
1 clove garlic	black olives

Skin the cod's roe, holding it in clingfilm or greaseproof paper to prevent your fingers getting too messy. Put it in a small bowl and cover with cold water. Leave to soak for 30 minutes to remove some of the saltiness, then drain it using a fine-meshed sieve and leave the sieve over the bowl for a few minutes to allow any excess water to drip out.

Remove the crusts from the bread and soak it in the milk for about 5 minutes until it becomes a spongy paste. Squeeze out any excess milk and put the bread in a food processor with the cod's roe, onion, crushed garlic and some freshly ground black pepper.

Process until the mixture forms a smooth paste, stopping occasionally to scrape down any bits from the sides of the bowl. Gradually pour in half the oil, with the machine running, as if you were making mayonnaise. Add the lemon juice, which should not amount to more than 2–3 tbsp, blend again and slowly add the rest of the oil. Garnish with the olives and serve with toast, warm pitta cut into fingers, or as a dip with crudités.

Smoked Mackerel Pâté

This is a quick and easy pâté to make, even more so if you have a food processor, in which case it takes literally seconds. Popular with children who often turn their noses up at whole fish, it can be used to fill rolls or sandwiches. As a more elegant starter, serve it in a pretty china dish, decorated with black olives and a slice or two of lemon, and hand wholemeal toast separately.

This quantity is enough for a generous starter for four to six people.

Makes 12 oz (335 g)

8 oz (225 g) smoked mackerel fillet	juice of 1 lemon
	½ level teaspoon cayenne
4 oz (110 g) curd cheese (medium-fat cream cheese)	

Pull the skin off the mackerel, break the fish into chunks and put it in the food processor. Add the other ingredients and blend till smooth. It has a pleasanter appearance and texture if you don't overprocess it, so that flecks of fish remain visible. If you are making the pâté by hand, mash the skinned fish well with a fork, before beating in the other ingredients.

Curd cheese is just like normal full-fat cream cheese in appearance but its lower fat content has obvious health advantages. If you want an even lighter cream cheese, there is one available made from skimmed milk, marketed under the brand name Quark.

Battenberg Fish Pâté

Sometimes it's fun to create visually attractive or unusual dishes and this pâté made from three differently coloured fish is certainly striking as well as tasting excellent. The final effect resembles a Battenberg cake, with two white squares, one pink and one yellow. Although it contains salmon, you don't need an awful lot, so I've included it in this section of the book, though you may prefer to make it on a rather more special occasion when you have guests coming round.

You will need a small rectangular terrine dish about 4½ x 3½ inches (11.5 x 9 cm) and 2 inches (5 cm) deep, and a food processor. Buy smoked haddock that has no artificial colour — if you think it's a bit pale when puréed, add a pinch of turmeric.

Serves 4–6

For the white part

8 oz (225 g) cod fillet	6 black peppercorns
1 oz (30 g) butter	¼ pint (150 ml) milk
½ medium onion	dash Tabasco sauce
1 clove garlic	1 tbsp lemon juice
2 tsp anchovy essence	**For the pink part**
1 tbsp lemon juice	5 oz (140 g) salmon steak
black pepper	¼ pint (150 ml) dry white wine
For the yellow part	bayleaf
5 oz (140 g) smoked haddock fillet	few slices onion
bayleaf	6–8 juniper berries or black
few slices onion	peppercorns

To make the white part   Skin the cod fillet and dice it fairly finely. Chop the ½ onion finely as well. Heat the butter in a frying pan and sauté the onion with the crushed garlic over a medium heat until soft. Add the cod and stir-fry over a more intense heat for 2–3 minutes until cooked. Cool slightly and purée in the food processor with the anchovy essence, lemon juice and some freshly ground black pepper. Put in the fridge to firm up slightly.

To make the yellow part   Skin the smoked haddock and put it in a saucepan with the bayleaf, few slices of onion, black peppercorns and enough milk to just cover, about ¼ pint (150 ml). Bring gently to the boil and then turn down the heat and poach until the fish is cooked, about 5 minutes. Lift out the haddock and purée it in the food processor with a dash of Tabasco sauce and the lemon juice. Refrigerate.

To make the pink part   Poach the salmon steak in the wine in a saucepan together with the bayleaf, few slices of onion and juniper berries (use black peppercorns if you have no stock of juniper berries). It will take about 5 minutes from coming to poaching point to cook through to the bone. Remove the salmon and reduce the cooking liquor to 1 tablespoon by fast boiling. Skin the fish and remove the central bone and any small ones in the V at the top of the steak, then purée the flesh with the strained cooking liquor in the food processor. Refrigerate.

When the three mixtures have firmed up a little, lightly oil the terrine dish. Divide the cod mixture into two and fill half the bottom of the dish

Battenberg Fish Pâté (page 63)

with one lot, lengthways, leaving an equal space alongside it where you can gently press in the pink mixture. For the second layer, use the remaining half of the cod to repeat the pattern diagonally opposite the first white square, and fill the last strip with the smoked haddock mixture.

Chill again for several hours. Just before serving, run a sharp knife round between the terrine dish and the pâté, invert it on to a plate, hold the two together and shake sharply from side to side. It should come out quite easily. Mop up any excess oil with a piece of kitchen paper and serve with wholemeal toast and a spoonful or two of mayonnaise.

Scallops with Jerusalem Artichokes

Coquilles Saint Jacques Parisienne, scallops served on the shell with a border of puréed potatoes, is one of the classic French dishes. But you need at least three scallops per shell to make a decent serving, which gets expensive when you are feeding four or more. Here is an alternative, using that much-neglected vegetable, the Jerusalem artichoke, which resembles a knobbly potato. Ask your fishmonger for the rounded half of the shells when you buy the scallops.

You will need a piping bag to make the potato border.

Serves 4

4 scallops plus 4 rounded shells	a little milk
12 oz (335 g) Jerusalem artichokes	12 oz (335 g) potatoes
½ pint (300 ml) dry white wine	2 oz (55 g) butter
bayleaf	1 oz (30 g) white flour
black peppercorns	seasoning
parsley stalks	1 tbsp grated Parmesan cheese
2 slices lemon	

Scrub the artichokes. If they are quite regular-shaped, peel them now, but the very knobbly ones are easier to peel after cooking. Cut them into chunks about 1 inch (2.5 cm) square and boil them in slightly salted water with a squeeze of lemon juice until cooked. Make sure they are really tender (this will take about 20 minutes), since undercooked they may cause indigestion. Remove them from the water and peel if you haven't already done so.

Cut the scallops off their flat shell and wash them under the cold tap to remove any sand. Poach them in the wine with the herbs, crushed black peppercorns and lemon slices for 3–4 minutes. Remove the scallops and cut them into two or three slices each. Strain the cooking liquor into a measuring jug, making it up to ½ pint (300 ml) with milk if necessary.

Grilled Red Mullet with Romesco Sauce (page 80) and Crab Mousse (page 100)

Peel, boil and mash the potatoes, making a smooth purée by adding a little milk and about 1 oz (30 g) butter. Season. Divide the scallops and artichoke chunks between the 4 rounded shells, which you must first scrub well in hot water. Pipe a border of puréed potato round the edges, using a starred nozzle.

Melt the rest of the butter in a non-stick pan, add the flour and cook for 30 seconds. Blend in the wine-milk mixture, stirring well, until thick. Taste for seasoning — you will find it may need a fair amount — and simmer for 5 minutes over a very low heat. Spoon the sauce over the scallops and artichokes, filling every crevice. Sprinkle with the Parmesan. You can now store the dish in the fridge, carefully covered with non-PVC clingfilm, until just before serving.

To serve, preheat the grill and slide the filled shells under it for about 10 minutes, until the potato ridges turn golden brown. Don't be impatient and take them out too early, or they will not have had time to heat through.

This starter is quite filling.

Curried Creamy Crab

This is a simple starter that looks good if served in scallop shells, but goes well on toast, too. If you use brown rice, you will have to put it on to cook some time before starting to prepare the rest of the dish. With white rice, which cooks more quickly, the whole thing can be done together.

Serves 4

4 oz (110 g) rice	½ pint (300 ml) milk
1 medium onion	seasoning
1 oz (30 g) butter	8 oz (225 g) white crabmeat
1 large clove garlic	squeeze lemon juice
1 tbsp wholemeal flour	2 tbsp fresh chopped parsley
1 tsp curry powder	

Put the rice on to cook. Chop the onion and sauté it in the butter in a medium-sized saucepan with the crushed garlic. After 5 minutes stir in the flour and curry powder and cook for a couple of minutes over a gentle heat. Add the milk gradually, stirring until the sauce is smooth. Season well.

Drain the rice (it should still have some 'bite' so don't overcook it), and stir it into the sauce. Add the crabmeat and a squeeze of lemon juice and mix gently. When the mixture is piping hot, pile it into 4 warmed scallop shells. Sprinkle with chopped parsley and serve.

Mussels au Gratin

This is a wonderful way to serve mussels, particularly for those who are slightly squeamish about eating them plainly steamed. You can prepare the dish a few hours in advance, up to the final grilling. Remember, though, that freshness is essential when eating shellfish, so keep them in salted water before scrubbing and store the prepared dish in the fridge until you are ready to flash it under the grill.

You may use white or brown breadcrumbs, but do not substitute margarine for the butter.

Serves 4

1 quart or 2 lb (900 g) mussels
1 tbsp olive oil
1 large clove garlic
½ medium onion
2 oz (55 g) soft butter

1 heaped tbsp fresh chopped
  parsley
black pepper
2 tbsp dried breadcrumbs
2 tbsp grated Parmesan cheese

Scrub the mussels, pulling off the beards and discarding any that do not close tightly when tapped. Put them in a large saucepan containing about 1 inch (2.5 cm) water, cover and bring to the boil. Simmer for 5 minutes until the shells have opened. Drain, and throw away any mussels that remain closed. Remove the top shell of each one and discard. Lay the half shells containing the orange flesh on a baking sheet or two shallow ovenproof dishes, open side up.

Chop the onion finely and sauté it with the crushed garlic in the oil in a small saucepan until soft. Cool slightly. Mix in the soft butter, parsley, black pepper and breadcrumbs. Spoon a little of the mixture into each half shell with a teaspoon and sprinkle the whole lot with grated Parmesan.

Grill the mussels under a high heat until the cheese browns slightly. Serve immediately, tackling them with a fork and teaspoon or a teaspoon and your fingers!

Moules Marinières

Everybody who loves shellfish is familiar with this simple yet renowned dish. Here is how to re-create that steaming bowl of blue-black mussels which, for me, epitomizes eating on the Continent. This quantity serves 4 as a starter or 2 as a main course, allowing fairly generous servings.

2 quarts or 4 lb (1.8 kg) mussels
½ pint (300 ml) water
2 glasses dry white wine
½ medium onion
2 slices lemon

black pepper
2 bayleaves
3 tbsp fresh chopped parsley
2 tbsp single cream (optional)

Clean the mussels in the usual way, using fine oatmeal as described on page 50 to cleanse them further and plump them up. Put them in a large saucepan and pour in the water and wine. Chop the onion roughly and add it, along with the lemon slices and bayleaves. Season with black pepper. Turn the mussels a few times with a large spoon and then cover the pan and bring the contents quickly to the boil. Simmer until the shells open, about 5 minutes. Shake the pan once or twice during cooking.

Ladle the mussels into soup plates, discarding any that have not opened. Sprinkle with the chopped parsley and pour most of the cooking liquor over them — the very bottom of the pan will contain some grit and sand, so leave that behind. If you wish you may add a little single cream to each bowl.

Put one large bowl in the centre of the table as a *poubelle* (dustbin) for the empty shells and tuck in, using a spoon and fork, or just your fingers. Mop up the juices with French bread.

Herring Roe Vol-au-Vents

These are good savouries to offer with drinks, or you could make enough to serve as a starter. Ready-made puff pastry, bought either fresh or frozen, is so good that I must confess I have given up making my own. In this case you can even buy the vol-au-vents ready cut out, so all you have to do is pop them in the oven and spoon in the filling. This quantity makes 6 medium-sized ones, small enough to hold in your fingers but, unlike the cocktail (or bouchée) size, not so small that you hardly get a taste of the creamy filling.

4 oz (110 g) herring roes
6 medium-sized uncooked vol-
    au-vent cases, frozen or
    homemade
beaten egg or 2 tbsp milk
¼ medium onion

½ oz (15 g) butter
1 tbsp double cream
1 heaped tsp wholemeal flour
dash Tabasco sauce
black pepper

Brush the vol-au-vent cases with beaten egg or milk. (If using frozen ones, you do not need to defrost them.) Place them on a wet baking tray and bake in a preheated oven at Gas 7/425°F/220°C for 10 minutes until golden brown. Cool, remove the lids and carefully scoop out the insides using a teaspoon.

Melt the butter in a small saucepan. Finely chop the onion and sauté it in the butter until soft. Add the chopped herring roe and cook gently, stirring occasionally, for about 5 minutes. Stir in the flour and cream, cook 1–2 minutes more until it thickens, and add the Tabasco and black pepper.

Spoon the filling into the vol-au-vent cases, replace the lids and reheat when needed at Gas 6/400°F/200°C for 5–10 minutes, uncovered.

Marinated Herring Fillets

Marinated herrings bought loose in delicatessens are never as good as homemade ones. Furthermore, you are never sure how old they are and therefore how soon you should eat them. Those preserved in brine in jars are not a patch on the real things which, as you will find if you follow this recipe, are delicious and much cheaper. They will keep in the fridge for up to a week.

Makes 12

6 fresh herrings
1 lemon
2 medium onions
Dijon or German mustard

¾ pint (425 ml) white wine vinegar
1 dsp juniper berries or black
    peppercorns
2 bayleaves

Ask your fishmonger to fillet the herrings. Wash them and pat dry so they will not be too slippery to handle. Slice each herring in two lengthways if the fish is still all in one piece. Slice the onions and the lemon.

Lay each fillet skin-side down and spread the inside with the mustard. Depending on your taste and the strength of the mustard, this can be a generous or meagre amount. Grasping the herring at the head end, roll it up towards the tail. This is a little fiddly, but it is much easier if you roll towards you. Secure each fillet with a couple of cocktail sticks. The plumper the herring, the more it will try and unroll — but the more delicious the end result!

Pack the rolls into a deep, non-metal dish, ideally not more than 6 inches (15 cm) across. Sprinkle the onions over the first layer, cover with a few lemon slices, a bayleaf and half the crushed juniper berries or peppercorns. Put in the second layer and repeat. Pour over the vinegar (you may need more than the given amount depending on the size of your dish), and put a small bowl containing a tin or something quite heavy on top of the herrings, to ensure the vinegar is covering the fish.

Cover the whole thing with clingfilm and leave in the fridge for two days before eating.

Oriental Mackerel Strips with Dip

A good dish to prepare in advance to serve with drinks. Use a low-fat 'cream' cheese, or half cream cheese and half natural set yoghurt. This quantity would make good nibbles for 6–8 people, served with a bowl of unsalted nuts or crudités. Rice wine vinegar can be found in Chinese stores.

2 medium really fresh mackerel
½–¾ pint (300–425 ml) rice
  wine vinegar

1¼ oz (50 g) tin anchovies
8 oz (225 g) low-fat cream cheese
a little milk

Ask the fishmonger to gut and bone the mackerel but keep them whole. Wash them well and open them out flat on the work surface. With a sharp knife cut across the width in narrow strips about ½–¾ inch (1.5–2 cm) wide. Put these in a glass bowl and pour the rice vinegar over. Marinate for at least 12 hours in the fridge, up to 24 will do no harm.

In a bowl or the food processor, mash the drained anchovies to a fine paste and beat in the cheese and a little milk. It should not be too stiff or you will not be able to dip in the mackerel pieces. Drain the fish, which should be 'cooked' by the acidity of the vinegar, and fold each piece in half, fastening the ends on to a cocktail stick. Serve with the dip.

Whitebait with Parmesan

I rarely fry fish, preferring other, lighter methods of cooking them, but crisp deep-fried whitebait make a terrific and very popular starter. The oil should reach 350–390°F (180–195°C) *before* you put in the fish. If you don't have a thermometer, you can gauge when the oil is ready by watching carefully for a slight blue haze that comes off it.

For four people it is best to cook the fish in two or more batches, as putting it in all at once not only produces a dangerous amount of bubbling (don't fill the pan more than half-full with oil anyway), but also causes the temperature to drop more than 50°F, which results in soggy fish.

If you don't have a deep frier, use a wok or shallow-fry the whitebait in smaller batches in a frying pan.

Serves 4

1 lb (450 g) small whitebait
3 tbsp grated Parmesan
2 tbsp wholemeal flour

seasoning
4 lemon wedges

Don't wash the whitebait, the whole point of this fish is that you eat *everything*! Heat the oil until just beginning to haze. Sprinkle the cheese and flour on a dinner plate, season well and quickly roll the fish in it before lowering them into the oil. Contrary to instinct, you should now turn the heat *up*, to return it to the right temperature to make the whitebait really crisp and golden. They only take 5 minutes. Remove with a slotted spoon and transfer to kitchen paper to absorb any oil, before serving on warmed plates with a wedge of lemon.

Don't coat the whitebait until just before cooking, or the moisture from the fish will turn the flour and cheese into a soggy, sticky casing.

Cheat's Blini and Caviar

The true version of this Russian hors d'oeuvre consists of crisp yeast pancakes and, of course, sturgeon's roe or caviar. Enough said. For those whose budgets don't stretch to this most expensive of fish roes and who hate working with yeast, this cheat's version does nonetheless prove very popular with friends. Trying to impress the boss might not be such a good idea! The blinis here are made from straightforward pancake batter, which of course gives a softer final result. Make sure you cook them really wafer thin, though.

Serves 4

2 oz (55 g) white flour, or
   ½ white ½ buckwheat
pinch salt
1 egg
¼ pint (150 ml) milk

¼ pint (150 ml) sour cream or
   natural yoghurt
½ medium onion
3 x 1¾ oz (50 g) pots black
   lumpfish roe
1 tbsp sunflower oil

Make the batter by sifting the flour into a mixing bowl with the salt. Make a well in the centre and drop in the egg. With an electric beater or wooden spoon, mix the egg into the flour and gradually pour in the milk, beating all the time until you have a smooth batter. Leave it to stand for 30 minutes.

Choose three small bowls — glass ones are good — which will look attractive on the table. Chop the onion and put this into one, pour the sour cream or natural yoghurt into another and empty the pots of lumpfish roe into the third. Provide napkins.

Heat the oil in a small 6 inch (15 cm) frying pan, then pour it out into a cup. Put a dessertspoon of batter into the pan, swirl it round so it thinly coats the bottom of the pan. As the pancake cooks, lift the edges with a spatula to loosen it. After about 2–3 minutes turn it over or toss it and cook the other side for a minute. Try and make the pancakes as crisp as possible without letting dark brown spots appear. Stack and keep warm until you have finished the batch, then serve — or if you are eating informally in the kitchen, you could serve them straight from the pan.

Main Courses

Yoghurt-Marinated Mackerel

The fresh tangy taste of ginger and orange and the clean sharpness of natural yoghurt cut through the slight oiliness which is characteristic of mackerel. Choose small fish, for the flesh is rich and filling and the huge mackerel seen sometimes on the fishmonger's slab are often too much for one person.

Serves 4

4 mackerel
1¼ inch (3 cm) piece fresh ginger
1 orange

2 small tubs (total 300 g) natural yoghurt
black pepper

Gut and wash the mackerel and remove the heads. Make 3 diagonal slashes in each side and place the fish side by side in a shallow dish or on a large plate. Peel the piece of ginger and chop it finely. Grate the rind from the orange. In a bowl mix together the orange rind, ginger and yoghurt and season with black pepper. Spoon the marinade over the fish, turning them over so both sides are coated. Make sure some gets inside the fish as well.

Leave for 2–3 hours. This is a fairly solid marinade, so you don't need to keep spooning it back over the mackerel. Then either bake the fish in the oven for 25–30 minutes at Gas 5/375°F/190°C or grill for 6–8 minutes each side. Check to see they are cooked through, as the time varies a little depending on the size of the fish, before serving garnished with slices of orange.

Grilled Mackerel with Gooseberry Sauce

Mackerel has a rich, rather oily flesh and needs a sharp sauce to counteract this. Fresh gooseberry sauce is perfect — here I have made it with fromage frais, now fairly widely available in good supermarkets, as a lighter, healthier 'creaming agent' than actual cream.

Serves 4

4 medium mackerel
¾ oz (20 g) butter
12 oz (335 g) fresh gooseberries

1 tbsp fromage frais
1 tbsp fresh chopped parsley

Gut the mackerel and wash well under running water. Make 2 or 3 slashes in each side, this helps the fish to cook more quickly.

With a small sharp knife, top and tail the gooseberries and put them in a small pan with the butter. Cook, covered, over a low heat until really soft — this will take about 10 minutes. Liquidize them and then press through a sieve to catch the pips. Return to the pan and beat in the fromage frais and the chopped parsley. You may want to add a little sugar, although I personally feel it doesn't need it.

Grill the mackerel for 6–8 minutes each side, depending on how big they are. The skin should be quite crisp. Serve with the sauce handed separately.

Mackerel and Apricot Kebabs with Barbecue Sauce

Mackerel is a good fish to use for kebabs, since the flesh is firm enough not to disintegrate and fall off the skewer as it cooks. In the summer, when fresh apricots are quite cheap, try this way of cooking them with mackerel over a barbecue in the garden. Pour the barbecue sauce over them on the plate or hand it separately. They can, of course, be grilled normally as well.

Serves 4

2 mackerel, about 1¼ lb (550 g) each
8 oz (225 g) button mushrooms
4 fresh apricots
1 oz (30 g) butter
black pepper
pinch thyme
Barbecue sauce
1 small onion
1 red pepper

1 tbsp sunflower oil
seasoning
juice of ½ lemon
2 dsp tomato purée
2 oz (55 g) soft brown sugar
1 level tbsp cornflour
2 tsp French mustard
1 tsp Worcestershire sauce
½ pint (300 ml) water

Ask your fishmonger to fillet the mackerel for you — you should end up with about 1½ lb (670 g) of fillets. Cut these into squares, not too small or they will split while cooking. The narrow tail end of the fillet can be folded over to make it thicker.

Halve the apricots and remove the stone, then quarter them. Remove the stalks from the mushrooms. Sauté them both together in the butter until the mushrooms have slightly turned colour and the apricots are a little softer. Cool while you make the Barbecue Sauce.

To do this, chop the onion and de-seeded red pepper very finely (in a food processor if you have one), and sauté gently in the oil. Combine the other ingredients in a bowl and mix well, adding the water last of all. Add this to the saucepan containing the onion and red pepper, stir and bring to the boil. Simmer for 5 minutes. Serve hot or cold.

Thread the mackerel, mushrooms and apricot quarters on to skewers — the quantities given here are sufficient for one 10 inch (25 cm) barbecue skewer per person, or two 5 inch (13 cm) butcher's meat skewers. Season with black pepper and sprinkle with a little thyme.

Grill or barbecue for 8–10 minutes, turning once, and serve immediately.

Skate with Orange and Caper Sauce

Skate has such a good flavour that it needs just a very simple sauce to accompany it. The classic 'black' butter sauce I find rather too greasy, so here I have used orange juice instead and added some finely sliced leek. A wing of skate weighs about 1½–2 lb (670–900 g) and is fairly meaty — almost like chicken breast, some claim.

Serves 4

1½–2 lb (670–900 g) skate wing
Court bouillon
2 pints (1.1 litres) water
1 tsp salt
4 tbsp white wine vinegar
½ onion (sliced)
bayleaf
parsley stalks
crushed black peppercorns

Sauce
1 medium leek
½ oz (15 g) butter
juice of 2 oranges
1 tbsp capers
1 tbsp fresh chopped parsley

Bring the ingredients for the court bouillon to the boil and simmer them for 15 minutes, then remove the pan from the heat. Meanwhile, wash the skate wing and divide it into 4 portions. Slice the leek and wash it in a sieve to remove any grit.

Put the skate pieces in a shallow flameproof dish or roasting tin and pour the court bouillon over them. Bring to the boil on top of the stove and then poach very gently for 20 minutes. The water should be shuddering rather than bubbling.

Heat the butter in a small saucepan and sauté the sliced leek until soft. Stir in the orange juice, capers and chopped parsley and season with black pepper. Remove the skate from the cooking liquor and scrape off the rather gelatinous skin on both sides with a knife. Pour the sauce over the skate and serve. The fan of bones, which are in fact cartilage, can be easily removed while eating the fish.

Plain boiled waxy potatoes and a vegetable like carrots or braised celery go very well with this dish.

Hake with Mussels

Hake is a neglected fish in Britain but in northern Spain, where it is very popular, they find a dozen different ways to cook it. This is an adaptation of a dish I tasted in the Rioja area, which combines the subtle flavours of mussels and mushrooms to make a delicious sauce.

The use of a good brand of shelled mussels in brine (not vinegar or sauce) is quite acceptable here, but note that the weight given below is without liquid.

Serves 4

4 hake steaks, 5–6 oz (140–170 g) each	3 oz (85 g) button mushrooms
½ pint (300 ml) fish stock	1 oz (30 g) butter
4 tbsp white Rioja	1 tbsp white flour
1 medium onion	4 oz (110 g) shelled mussels
black peppercorns	seasoning
bayleaf	1 tbsp fresh chopped parsley

Put the fish steaks in a shallow gratin dish and pour the wine and fish stock round. Chop the onion and sprinkle it over the top of the fish, add the bayleaf and black peppercorns. Poach in an oven preheated to Gas 4/350°F/180°C for 15–20 minutes until the fish is cooked. Since it is to be kept hot while you make the sauce, and therefore will cook a little more, do not overdo it at this stage.

Meanwhile finely chop the mushrooms. If you are using fresh mussels, bring them to the boil in a large pan with a little water, wine and seasoning and simmer until the shells open. Remove from the shell.

When the fish is ready, keep it hot while you make the sauce. Strain the cooking liquor into a measuring jug (you should have about ½ pint/ 300 ml). Melt the butter in a non-stick pan, add the flour to make a roux and pour on the stock, stirring well to make a smooth sauce. Stir in the mussels and chopped mushrooms and simmer for 5 minutes. Test for seasoning and pour over the fish.

Serve sprinkled with the chopped parsley.

Grilled Herring with Rhubarb Sauce

Herring is a fairly oily fish, so this tart sauce is ideal to serve with it. Unless you have a really sweet tooth, the sauce shouldn't need any sugar. Bear in mind that it is not supposed to be as sweet as it would be if you were serving rhubarb for dessert, or it would not counteract the richness of the herring so well.

This is a cheap dish which is very quick to prepare.

Serves 4

4 herrings, about 8 oz (225 g) each
8 oz (225 g) rhubarb
1 tbsp water
1½–2 tbsp natural yoghurt

Wash the rhubarb, trim the ends and cut it into 1 inch (2.5 cm) pieces. Put these in a saucepan with the water, cover with a lid and cook over a gentle heat, stirring occasionally. After 20 minutes it will be very soft and much reduced in size.

Meanwhile gut the herrings and cut off their heads. Score them twice on each side and grill for 4–5 minutes, turn them over and give them another 4–5 minutes. Mash the rhubarb and whisk in the yoghurt, using a small balloon whisk, until smooth. Heat the sauce through without boiling, or the yoghurt will curdle, and serve with the grilled herrings.

Herrings in Oatmeal with Mustard Sauce

This traditional Scottish dish makes an excellent and cheap supper or brunch, served with grilled bacon and tomatoes. If you prefer, you can grill the fish as well, rather than frying them.

Serves 4

4 herrings, about 8 oz (225 g) each
1 egg
2–3 oz (55–85 g) coarse oatmeal
seasoning
If frying
2–3 oz (55–85 g) butter

Ask the fishmonger to gut and fillet the herring, or do them yourself, giving two fillets per person. Break the egg over a large plate and whisk it lightly with a fork. Scatter the oatmeal over another plate or board and season it with the salt and pepper. Coat both sides of each fillet with the beaten egg and then press well into the oatmeal until firmly coated. Fry in the hot fat, or grill. Serve with mustard sauce (see page 183).

Many people omit the egg but I then find that unless the fish are very fresh, virtually straight from the sea, the oatmeal does not stick to the fillets so densely.

Trout Baked with White Wine

Fresh trout is delicious served absolutely plain. Grilling rather spoils its delicate flesh and dries it out. Instead, try this way of baking trout in the oven. Wrapped in protective silver foil and surrounded by a little white wine, the fish cooks gently and evenly in just a few minutes. Make sure, though, that there are no holes in the foil, or the juices and wine will leak out.

This is also the best way to cook trout if you are going to serve it cold, since the flesh stays wonderfully moist, yet firm enough to skin when cool.

Serves 4

4 trout	4 bayleaves
2 oz (55 g) butter	black pepper
1 lemon	½ pint (300 ml) dry white wine

Gut the trout if you have bought them whole and hold them under cold running water, belly uppermost, to wash out any stubborn pieces of intestine. Make sure you remove the dark strip of blood running along the inner side of the backbone, by rubbing it with your thumb, or the cooked flesh will taste muddy.

Take a piece of silver foil at least 6 inches (15 cm) longer and wider than the fish. Grease it with a small knob of butter and leave the remains of this knob on the foil when you have finished. Put two slices of lemon and a bayleaf in the belly of the fish and season with black pepper. Place the prepared trout on the greased foil and bring up the ends and sides to form an open envelope. Pour in about 5 tbsp white wine and seal the envelope by turning the edges over a few times and crumpling them tightly. The ends should be a few inches off the work surface. Repeat with the other fish.

Place the wrapped trout on a baking tray and cook in a preheated oven at Gas 6/400°F/200°C for 15–20 minutes. If the fish are lying very close together the centre ones will take a little longer to cook. Unwrap and serve with a baked potato and salad. Put a large plate in the centre for everyone to use for the discarded head and bones.

Trout Stuffed with Watercress and Fennel

Serves 4

4 trout	seasoning
2 medium fennel 'bulbs'	juice of ½ lemon
1 bunch watercress	2 tbsp wholemeal flour
2 oz (55 g) butter	1 tbsp sunflower oil

Ask the fishmonger to gut the fish and remove the bone from the *inside* —it is important that the fish remain in one piece or the stuffing will spill out. When you start preparing the dish, cut off the fins as well as trimming the tail into a neat V-shape. Cut off the head just behind the gills.

Trim the root from the fennel and cut off the thick stalks, as these tend to be rather spongy. Wash the watercress under cold running water and cut off most of the stalk. Chop the fennel with the watercress in a food processor (being careful not to reduce them to a purée), or by hand. Soften them in half the butter in a saucepan for 10 minutes, over a gentle heat. Season and stir in the lemon juice.

Sprinkle the flour, seasoned with a pinch of salt and some freshly ground black pepper, on to a large plate and lay the fish on it, coating both sides. Knock off any excess flour and open each fish out, skin side down. Spread the stuffing on one half and fold the other back on top.

Melt the remaining butter with the oil in a large frying pan (the oil prevents the butter from burning) and, when hot, fry the fish on both sides until golden brown. Gently lift up the top fillet to check the flesh is cooked through, and serve.

Bhutanese Trout

This recipe was passed on to me by my cousin, who claims he was told it by a Bhutanese prince during his travels in India. Whatever its rather obscure origins, it is a deliciously simple way of making the most of a really fresh trout.

Serves 2

2 trout	large pinch cayenne
2 limes	1 oz (30 g) butter
wholemeal flour	1 tbsp sunflower oil

Gut the trout if necessary and cut off the head and tail — this is so they fit in the frying pan, more than anything else. Put them in a shallow dish with the juice of the two limes, plus any bits of lime flesh left on the squeezer. Leave for 8–12 hours, depending on your day's schedule, turning occasionally. Make sure the lime juice gets inside the belly of the fish as well.

After this time remove the trout from the marinade, which you should keep on one side. The citric acid will have partially or completely 'cooked' the flesh — the length of time the trout need to be fried in the butter will vary, depending on how 'cooked' they are at this stage.

Heat the butter and oil in a frying pan. Meanwhile sprinkle 1–2 tablespoons of flour on a plate with a large pinch of cayenne. Coat the fish in this then shake them to remove any excess flour. Fry for 5–8 minutes each side and dish up. Pour away the fat and add the lime marinade to the pan. Swirl it around over a high heat and pour it over the fish.

Grilled Red Mullet with Romesco Sauce

Red mullet responds well to being simply grilled and this spicy Spanish sauce helps to bring out all the aromatic flavours of the Mediterranean.

Serves 4

4 red mullet, each about 8–10 oz (225–280 g)	1 large clove garlic
3–4 tbsp red wine	6 blanched almonds
3–4 tbsp olive oil	6 blanched hazelnuts
rosemary	pinch salt
Sauce	½ tsp cayenne
2 ripe tomatoes	¼ pint (300 ml) olive oil
	1 tbsp wine vinegar

Ask the fishmonger to scale and gut the fish but to leave in the dark brown liver that gives red mullet its popular, slightly gamey flavour. Cut off the fins and score two diagonal cuts on either side of each fish. Put them in a dish and sprinkle with the wine, oil and rosemary. Leave for about an hour, turning once.

To make the sauce, peel the garlic and put it on a small greased tray with the tomatoes in an oven preheated to Gas 4/350°F/170°C for 25 minutes. Five minutes before the end add the nuts (if you can't find blanched hazelnuts, boil shelled ones for a couple of minutes and scrape off the skins). Cool and skin the tomatoes.

Put the garlic and nuts in a food processor or liquidi r and grind them as finely as possible. Add the tomatoes, a little salt and the cayenne. Purée these together and gradually add the oil, as if you were making mayonnaise. Finish with the vinegar. Leave to stand for a few hours and you will find it thickens up well. (This sauce is also excellent with shellfish and baked fish.)

Preheat the grill, lift the mullet out of their marinade and grill them for about 5 minutes each side. Be careful not to overcook, or the flesh quickly goes dry. Serve with the Romesco sauce.

Red Mullet Stuffed with Spinach and Mushrooms

Serves 4

4 red mullet, weighing about
  8–10 oz (225–280 g) each
8 oz (225 g) fresh spinach
4 oz (110 g) button mushrooms

1½ oz (45 g) butter
seasoning
freshly grated nutmeg
pinch thyme

Gut the mullet and remove the gills, scale thoroughly and cut off the
fins. Wash the spinach very well in a sinkful of cold water, snapping off
the stalks. Put it into a saucepan without any extra water and cook for 5
minutes, stirring occasionally, until it has much reduced in size. Squeeze
it dry between two plates to remove as much water as possible.

Finely chop the mushrooms and sauté them in ½ oz (15 g) of the
butter for a few minutes. Chop the spinach and stir it into the
mushrooms. Season well and add a pinch of thyme and a little freshly
grated nutmeg. Fill the cavities of the fish with the stuffing.

Preheat the oven to Gas 6/400°F/200°C. Taking the remaining butter,
grease 4 pieces of silver foil, leaving a small knob of butter on each
piece. Lay the fish on top and wrap tightly. Place on a baking sheet and
bake for 15 minutes in the oven until cooked.

This goes particularly well with brown rice.

Rosemary-Baked Red Mullet with Provençal Sauce

Here is a recipe for red mullet that takes it back to its Mediterranean
origins. Fresh rosemary, which can easily be grown in an English garden
(and dried for the winter) gives off the most wonderful aroma while
baking, which it imparts to the fish. The provençal sauce includes
pungent black olives.

Serves 4

4 red mullet, weighing about
  8–10 oz (225–280 g) each
3 tbsp olive oil
3 cloves garlic
3 x 6 inch (15 cm) sprigs
  fresh rosemary
4 slices lemon
black pepper
Provençal sauce
1 tbsp olive oil

2 cloves garlic
2 oz (55 g) black olives
1 lb 12 oz (785 g) tin tomatoes
1 tsp fresh rosemary, chopped
pinch each dried basil and thyme
bayleaf
black pepper
3 tbsp red wine

Descale the fish thoroughly and trim the fins. Gut the fish but leave the
dark liver inside. Take a heavy casserole with a large base and pour in

the 3 tbsp of oil. Peel and slice the garlic cloves and sprinkle them on the bottom of the casserole. Put in two of the rosemary sprigs, then lay the cleaned fish on top. Lay another sprig of rosemary over the fish with the lemon slices, and season with black pepper. Cover with the lid and bake in a preheated oven at Gas 5/375°F/190°C for 20–30 minutes, basting with the hot oil once.

Meanwhile make the sauce. Heat the oil in a saucepan, add the crushed garlic and sauté for 5 minutes while you stone and halve the olives. Pour in the tinned tomatoes and crush them well, then add the olives, herbs and wine and season with black pepper. You may find the olives provide enough of a salty taste without adding any extra salt. Cover and simmer for 15–20 minutes.

Lift the fish from its bed of rosemary and serve with the sauce.

Stuffed Grey Mullet with Fennel Sauce

I do think it's worth removing the bone for this dish, which you can ask your fishmonger to do. However it's not difficult if you have a small sharp knife. A good dish made from a much underrated fish.

Serves 4

2 x 1 lb (450 g) grey mullet
8 oz (225 g) fennel bulb
½ oz (15 g) butter
2 cloves garlic
2 tbsp dried breadcrumbs
1 glass dry white wine
2 tbsp fresh chopped parsley
seasoning
bayleaf
lemon slices

Fennel sauce
1 oz (30 g) butter
1 oz (30 g) white flour
¼ pint (150 ml) fish stock
¼ pint (150 ml) dry white wine
2½ fl.oz (75 ml) milk
1 tsp fennel seeds
seasoning

Gut and scale the fish thoroughly. Laying each one belly side down on a board, press down hard with the heel of your hand along the backbone. This helps ease it away from the flesh. Turn over, snip each end of the bone and with a sharp knife, using short strokes, remove it from each fish. (Apart from the rib bones, there is a central ridge along the top of the vertebrae.) The fish must stay whole. Cut off the fins and trim the tail.

Trim the fennel bulb, remove the core and chop it very finely (a food processor will do this in seconds). Sweat it in the butter with the crushed garlic for 10 minutes. Soak the breadcrumbs in 2 tbsp of the wine and then stir them into the fennel with the parsley and some seasoning.

Stuff the fish with this mixture and bake them wrapped in silver foil with a bayleaf, some lemon slices and the rest of the wine in an oven preheated to Gas 4/350°F/180°C for 20 minutes. For the sauce, make a roux with the butter and flour and mix in the wine and stock, stirring well till smooth. Add the milk, fennel seeds and some seasoning and cook gently for about 5–10 minutes. It should not be very thick. Keep the sauce warm until the fish is ready, then serve it either poured over the mullet, or in a warmed sauceboat.

Grey Mullet with Leek Sauce

Serves 4

2 x 1 lb (450 g) grey mullet
8 oz (225 g) leeks, weighed after
  trimming
½ oz (15 g) butter
seasoning

pinch dried thyme
7½ fl.oz (225 ml) fish stock
1 tbsp low-fat cream cheese
squeeze lemon juice
2 heaped tsp cornflour

Gut the mullet and scale them thoroughly, then bone them keeping the fish in one piece. Slice the leeks fairly finely and wash them well in a colander under cold running water to remove any grit. Heat the butter in a saucepan and sweat the leeks with a pinch of thyme and some seasoning for about 10 minutes until quite soft, but do not cook them too long or they lose their bright green colour.

Liquidize the leeks with the fish stock and push this through a sieve, leaving about 2 tbsp of thick leek purée behind in the sieve. Mix the cream cheese with this purée, season with black pepper and a squeeze of lemon juice and push it into the belly cavities of the fish. Wrap in some oiled silver foil and bake in a preheated oven for 20–25 minutes at Gas 4/350°F/180°C until the fish are done.

When the fish are almost ready to serve, add the cornflour to the sieved sauce, season and reheat it to boiling point, stirring until thick. Add a squeeze of lemon juice and serve poured over the fish.

Trevally Stuffed with Cream Cheese and Capers

Trevally, or jack, is not a common fish, but worth buying when you see it. The flesh, being meaty and filling, rather like mackerel, is enhanced by the sharp taste of the capers in this recipe. This stuffing also goes well with red snapper. Both these fish are imported frozen, so make sure they are thoroughly defrosted before starting on the preparation.

Serves 4

1 whole trevally, about 2 lb (900 g)	1 tbsp capers
	2 tbsp lemon juice
6 oz (170 g) Quark or other low-fat soft cheese	seasoning
	½ glass dry white wine

Gut the fish if necessary, making sure you scrape out the dark blood along the backbone, which gives a bitter taste if cooked. Cut off the sharp fins and trim the tail. Leave the head on, but trim off the gills.

Chop the capers and mix them with the cream cheese, lemon juice and seasoning. Fill the cavity of the fish with the stuffing, pushing it in well to make sure it fills every gap. Lay the fish on a piece of buttered silver foil and bring up the sides. Pour in the white wine, then wrap the fish in the foil, securing it tightly enough to ensure the stuffing will not ooze out of the fish. Bake for 45–50 minutes at Gas 6/400°F/200°C.

Whole Stuffed Plaice

One winter, at dusk, I caught a flounder using a rod off a pebble beach in Sussex. Within an hour I was eating it poached and was surprised by its light yet pleasant flavour.

Both flounder, which is considered dull-tasting, and its cousin plaice, dismissed by many as poor man's food fit only for disguising in breadcrumbs and deep-frying, are somewhat underrated. Of course, they can't compare to other flat fish such as turbot or Dover sole, but for a cheap, healthy and light meal, baked or poached plaice fits the bill nicely. This recipe involves little preparation, as the fish comes to the table whole and you remove the central bone as you eat.

Serves 2

2 whole plaice, each weighing about 10 oz (280 g)	2 rashers bacon
	2 tbsp dried breadcrumbs
½ oz (15 g) butter	2½ fl.oz (75 ml) dry white wine
½ medium onion	seasoning
½ stick celery	2 oz (55 g) peeled prawns

If you like you can remove the dark skin from the plaice, but you can just as well serve it as it is and remove the skin while you are eating.

Make a cut in the fish from head to tail down the backbone on the dark skin side and, using your sharp filleting knife, loosen the flesh from the bones on this side in two fillets, leaving them still attached to the skeleton and fins along each side. This forms a pocket for the stuffing. With a pair of scissors, cut through the backbone at 2 inch (5 cm) intervals, so you can lift it out easily later. Lightly grease two large pieces of foil and lay the fish on them, pocket side up.

Chop the onion and celery and dice the bacon. Soften them in the butter in a small saucepan. Soak the breadcrumbs in about 2 tbsp white wine until they have swelled slightly, then stir them into the vegetables and bacon with the prawns and some seasoning.

Spoon the stuffing into the pocket you have made in each fish. Cover the top with a smaller piece of silver foil, then fold the edges up to seal, after pouring in a dash of white wine to keep the fish moist while cooking. Place on a large baking tray and bake in a preheated oven at Gas 6/400°F/200°C for 15–20 minutes depending on how thick the fish is.

Serve as they are, or you may cut off the head and tail first. Place a bowl in the centre of the table to put the bones in as you go.

Barbecued Stuffed Sardines in Vine Leaves

The first time I ate fresh sardines we bought them straight from the boat and grilled them over a fire on a Spanish beach. However many ways I have cooked them since, I still think that the flavours imparted from an open fire or barbecue suit them best.

In this recipe I have boned the sardines, which is quite easy, and then stuffed them with an aromatic fennel and Pernod mixture, before wrapping them in vine leaves to hold in the stuffing while cooking. The result is more than worth the extra preparation time and minus their many bones they are much simpler to eat al fresco.

The recipe is perfectly suitable for indoor grilling, but will lack that special final outdoor taste! Choose large sardines, weighing about 4 oz (110 g) each, as this cuts down on preparation time.

Serves 6

3 lb (1.35 kg) sardines (at least 2 per head)	1 tbsp olive oil
4 oz (110 g) vine leaves in brine	large pinch rosemary
2 pints (1.1 litre) fish stock or water	seasoning
	2 tbsp dried wholemeal breadcrumbs
8 oz (225 g) fennel bulb	1 tbsp Pernod
	1 tbsp water

The vine leaves take the longest to prepare for their final use, although this is 90 per cent cooking time rather than involving you directly. So first open the packet in which you bought them, drain them into a large bowl and pour boiling water over. Leave for 20 minutes while you start to deal with the sardines, then drain them again, put them into cold fresh water and leave for a further 20 minutes. Finally, simmer them in the fish stock (or water) for 35 minutes, drain and leave to dry out a little.

While all that is going on, scale and gut the sardines and remove the central bone, leaving the fish in one piece, as described on page 38.

(The tail should be left on as well this time, since then it can stick out of the vine-leaf parcel and give a fishy clue to what's inside.) This will take about 30–40 minutes, depending on how practised you are. Set the fish on one side.

Cut the rather spongy stalks off the top of the fennel, remove the hard core and chop the bulb very finely, in a food processor if you have one. Heat the oil in a small saucepan and sweat the fennel with the crushed garlic and rosemary until soft. Soak the breadcrumbs in the Pernod and water and stir them into the fennel with a pinch of salt and some freshly ground black pepper.

Open up the sardines and lay a line of stuffing (about 1–2 tsp) down the centre of each fish. Fold the fish over to its normal shape and roll it up in one or two vineleaves, depending on size, making sure the belly is well covered to prevent the stuffing oozing out. Refrigerate until ready to cook.

On a hot barbecue or under a preheated grill, the sardines will take 3–4 minutes each side. (Turn them over carefully with a pair of tongs.) When the vineleaves have started to turn black, the inside will be ready. As the leaves have been previously cooked, you can eat the whole thing.

Serve with a large salad and some robust red wine.

Oriental Fish Steaks

This is a fairly pungent sauce, so don't attempt the recipe using expensive halibut, or delicate sole fillets, as their superior flavour will be wasted. Hake, which can be rather bland, is certainly livened up by it however, and a good cod steak has enough character to stand up to the sweet-sour mixture.

Hoisin sauce, a Chinese barbecue sauce, can be bought ready-made in jars or cans in many supermarkets — Sharwood's is a good brand to look for.

Serves 4

4 hake or cod steaks	juice of 1 orange
4 spring onions	2 tbsp Hoisin sauce
2 tbsp clear honey	¼ tsp chilli powder
4 tbsp water	

Finely chop the spring onions and mix them with the honey, water, orange juice, Hoisin sauce and chilli powder. Arrange the fish steaks in an ovenproof dish and pour the sauce over about 30 minutes before you aim to start cooking them. (If you use non-clear honey, you will have to heat the sauce slightly first, to melt the honey.)

Preheat the oven to Gas 5/375°F/190°C. Bake the fish for 15–20 minutes and serve with rice.

Casseroled Herrings

This is a simple fish casserole with no pretensions, just the distinctive flavour of fresh herring. Sliced potatoes are cooked in the casserole as well to soak up the tasty juice. If you are serving this to people who are fussy about picking their fish off the bones, ask the fishmonger to fillet the herring for you first.

Serves 4

4–6 herring, depending on size	3 tinned anchovy fillets
¾ pint (425 ml) water	1½ lb (670 g) potatoes
2 tbsp white wine vinegar	2 tbsp sunflower oil
pinch ground allspice	seasoning
2–3 blades mace	pinch dried thyme
black peppercorns	2 tbsp fresh chopped parsley
1½ medium onions	

Put the water, vinegar, allspice, mace and crushed black peppercorns into a small saucepan. Chop half an onion and slice the anchovy fillets and add these. Bring to the boil and simmer, covered, for 20 minutes. Strain and keep the liquid.

Scrub and thickly slice the potatoes — they should be at least ¾ inch (2 cm) thick or they will disintegrate during cooking. Slice the remaining onion. Cut the heads and tails off the herring.

Heat the oil in a thick-bottomed flameproof casserole. (Le Creuset is ideal since you can bring it straight to the table for serving.) Sauté the sliced onion, then add the herring, layered with the potato slices. Season well and pour on the strained stock. Add the thyme, cover and bring to the boil. Simmer covered for 15 minutes, or bake in a preheated oven for 25–30 minutes at Gas 4/350°F/180°C.

Sprinkle with parsley before serving.

Fisherman's Sardines

A simple dish from the Mediterranean, this uses two of the essentials in a fisherman's life — fresh fish and coarse red wine.

Serves 4

2 lb (900 g) sardines	parsley stalks
2 large onions	bayleaf
2 large cloves garlic	seasoning
1 tbsp olive oil	juice of ½ lemon
½ bottle cheap red wine	1 oz (30 g) butter
few sprigs fresh thyme or pinch dried	1 tbsp white flour
	1 tbsp fresh chopped parsley

Scale the sardines in the usual way, working towards the head. Gut them carefully and remove the heads, tails, and fins. This is a little fiddly but well worth it. Slice the onions, heat the oil in a large flat-bottomed casserole or frying pan with lid, and soften the onions and crushed garlic for 10 minutes. Put in the herbs, add the wine, bring it to the boil and season well. Lay the prepared sardines on top of this, lower the heat and simmer, covered, for 5–10 minutes.

After this time carefully remove the sardines with a slotted spoon and arrange them in two rows down a serving platter. Squeeze over the lemon juice and keep warm. Strain the wine into a jug and make a roux in a saucepan with the butter and flour. Gradually add the wine, stirring all the time, and simmer until the sauce has thickened. If it is too thick, add a little water.

Pour the sauce over the fish and sprinkle with the chopped parsley. Serve with a crisp green salad, which includes some quite bitter items like curly endive or chicory, and a basket of French bread to mop up the rich purple-coloured sauce.

Squid in Red Wine

In this dish the squid are braised at length in a low oven. The resulting sauce is superb, it tastes more like a Boeuf Bourguignon gravy than simple red wine. Once you have cleaned the squid (buy large ones to make this quicker) it takes just a few minutes to put the dish together. After 1½ hours in the oven it will be transformed.

Serves 4

3 lb (1.35 kg) whole squid
2 medium onions
4 cloves garlic
2 tbsp olive oil
pinch salt
2 tbsp wholemeal flour

¾ pint (425 ml) full-bodied red wine
¼ pint (150 ml) water
black pepper
pinch each dried rosemary, thyme
  and oregano
bayleaf

Clean the squid in the usual way, leave the tentacles whole unless very large, and slice the bodies into rings.

Slice the onions and sauté them for 5 minutes in the olive oil with the garlic, using a flameproof, heavy-bottomed casserole. Add the squid and a pinch of salt and sauté over a high heat. The squid will produce quite a bit of liquid — continue cooking until this has all but evaporated, then mix in the flour. Stir in the wine and water. Season with black pepper and the herbs and transfer the casserole to the middle of the oven at Gas 3/325°F/170°C for 1½ hours.

Serve with rice.

Stuffed Squid

You need to buy squid whose tubular bodies are at least 5 inches (13 cm) long for this dish, or it becomes rather fiddly to prepare. A quick and non-messy way to get the moist stuffing into the cleaned squid is to use a piping bag and nozzle — just squeeze some into each tube in a matter of seconds. If you want, you can serve this dish cold as an hors d'oeuvre, in which case cook it in a low oven in olive oil, rather than in the tomato sauce given here.

Serves 4

12 medium-sized squid (1¼ lb/
  550 g minimum)
1½ medium onions
2 cloves garlic
2 tbsp olive oil
8 oz (225 g) mushrooms
6 tbsp fresh wholemeal
  breadcrumbs
4 tbsp dry white wine
seasoning
1 tbsp fresh chopped parsley

Tomato sauce
1 tbsp olive oil
1 clove garlic
1 medium onion
14 oz (390 g) tin tomatoes
¼ pint (150 ml) dry white wine
pinch rosemary, pinch basil
2 tsp tomato purée
seasoning
bayleaf

Clean the squid as shown on page 54. Keep the bodies whole, chop the tentacles finely and put them in a bowl on one side. To make the stuffing, finely chop 1½ onions and sauté them in 2 tbsp oil with the crushed garlic in a small saucepan until soft. Add the mushrooms, also finely chopped (you can use a food processor to speed up these two operations) and cook until they have reduced in size and have produced a bit of juice. Stir in the breadcrumbs, which you have moistened in the wine, and add the chopped parsley. Season and cool.

Prepare the sauce in which the squid are to be cooked by softening the onion, sliced, in the oil with the crushed garlic. Stir in the tin of tomatoes, breaking them up well with a fork or potato masher, together with the seasoning, tomato purée, wine and herbs. Simmer gently while you stuff the squid.

Using a piping bag with nozzle, a small teaspoon or your fingers, push the stuffing right down into the squid bodies. Fill only three-quarters of each tube, as they puff up during cooking and over-stuffing will cause them to burst. Fasten the opening with a wooden cocktail stick. Lay the squid in the tomato sauce, cover and simmer for 15–20 minutes over a low heat. Serve with brown rice.

If you wish to eat the squid cold, an attractive way to serve them, after stewing them gently in olive oil, is to allow them to cool and then to slice them using a really sharp knife. The slices, about an inch (2.5 cm) thick, look good arranged on a bed of shredded lettuce and radicchio.

Aubergine Stuffed with Crab and Walnuts

Choose aubergines that are smooth and shiny — slight wrinkles mean they are past their best. Here I have stuffed them with half-white, half-brown crabmeat, but for a cheaper and richer-tasting dish you could use all brown.

Serves 4

2 large aubergines
salt
1 medium onion
1 tbsp olive oil
1 clove garlic
4 oz (110 g) white crabmeat
4 oz (110 g) brown crabmeat
2 oz (55 g) shelled walnuts

4 medium tomatoes
4 tbsp dry white wine
1 tbsp fresh chopped mint or
    1 tsp dried
pinch dried thyme
black pepper
1 tbsp fresh chopped parsley

Cut the aubergines in half lengthways and scoop out most of the flesh, leaving about ¾ inch (1.5 cm) round the edge and bottom. Salt the shells well on the inside and leave upside-down in a colander. This brings out the bitter juices. Keep half of the scooped-out flesh and salt this well too.

Chop the onion and sauté it in the olive oil with the crushed garlic until golden brown. After the aubergines have been left salting for 30 minutes, wash them and the reserved flesh and pat dry. Chop the flesh and stir it into the onion, together with the crabmeat, chopped walnuts, chopped tomatoes, wine and herbs. Season with black pepper and cook gently for 5 minutes.

Cool the stuffing mixture slightly and then pile it into the aubergine shells. Wrap them in separate parcels of oiled silver foil and bake in a low oven, heated to Gas 3/325°F/170°C, for 40 minutes. Remove from the foil, sprinkle with chopped parsley and serve with brown rice.

Curried Monkfish with Cucumber

Monkfish has the terrific advantage of not disintegrating when cooked, so it doesn't lose its identity in this curry sauce. The cucumber with dill has a refreshing flavour that accompanies a curry well, although I have kept this one mild — add extra chilli if you like yours fiery! Monkfish fluctuates quite considerably in price, but is good value for money since with just one central bone there is very little wastage.

Serves 4

1¼–1½ lb (550–670 g) monkfish	½ pint (300 ml) fish stock
Curry sauce	bayleaf
1 tbsp sunflower oil	seasoning
½ medium onion	juice of half a lemon
1 tsp ground coriander	1 heaped tsp cornflour
½ tsp ground cumin	**Accompaniment**
¼ tsp each of ground ginger,	1½ cucumbers
turmeric and chilli powder	1 tbsp chopped fresh dill or
1 tsp tomato purée	1 tsp dried dillweed
1 glass dry white wine	½ oz (15 g) butter

To make the sauce, finely chop the onion and sauté it in the oil in a non-stick saucepan for about 5 minutes until golden brown. Add the spices and tomato purée and cook for a minute or two to absorb the oil. Pour in the wine and fish stock, stirring well to blend in the spices and tomato. Add the lemon juice, seasoning and bayleaf. Bring to the boil, cover and simmer for 20 minutes.

Prepare the cucumber by topping and tailing it and then cutting into quarters lengthways. Slice the quarters into 1 inch (2.5 cm) chunks and sauté them in the butter until tender, about 10 minutes, covering the pan and shaking it frequently. Sprinkle with fresh dill and they are ready to serve. If you are using dried dill, add it before you start to cook the cucumber.

Remove the central bone from the monkfish and cut the flesh into 2 inch (5 cm) pieces. Drop these into the curry sauce, and simmer until cooked, about 5 minutes. Stir in the cornflour, dissolved in about 3 tbsp of cold water until the sauce has thickened. Serve immediately with brown rice.

Monkfish and Sweet Pepper Pasta Sauce

Monkfish flesh is firm and does not fall to pieces when it is stirred around, which makes it ideal for this pasta sauce. Accompany it with a crisp green salad.

Serves 4

12 oz (335 g) monkfish	1 green pepper
1 tbsp olive oil	4 tbsp dry white wine
1 clove garlic	seasoning
½ onion	2½ fl.oz (75 ml) single cream
3 crisp stalks celery	2 tbsp fresh chopped parsley
1 red pepper	

Chop the onion and de-seed and chop the peppers. Slice the celery. Heat the oil in a saucepan and sauté the onion and garlic for a few minutes, add the peppers and celery and leave them to cook gently for about 5 minutes. Remove the central bone from the monkfish and dice the flesh into ½ inch (1.5 cm) pieces. Stir these into the pan with the white wine, season, cover and leave to cook for a further 3 minutes. Stir in the cream, sprinkle with the chopped parsley and serve over green spaghetti or pasta shapes.

End-of-Weekend Pasta Sauce

There comes a time in everybody's week when the cupboard is truly bare and we are forced to rummage around at the back of the fridge to concoct something appetizing for supper. This is a quick pasta sauce made from vegetables found in the salad box, with a side raid on the freezer to supply the prawns. If you happen to be far-sighted enough to keep a small bag of shelled scallops in the freezer, then you can have a real feast.

Serves 2

6 oz (170 g) frozen peeled prawns	3 oz (85 g) button mushrooms
1 oz (30 g) butter	1 tsp tomato purée
½ medium onion	2 tbsp single cream
½ large green pepper	6–8 oz (170–225 g) pasta spirals
seasoning	

Defrost the prawns and pat them dry. Chop the onion and de-seed and slice the green pepper. Slice the mushrooms. Melt the butter in a small saucepan and soften the onion and green pepper for 5 minutes. Add the mushrooms, season well and cook for a further 5 minutes. Stir in the prawns, tomato purée and cream, heat through and pour over bowls of steaming pasta.

Quick-Fry Prawns with Red Pepper

This is an ideal dish when you are short of time and not feeling much like cooking, since it is so quick and easy to prepare. The bright colours and the fresh taste of the ginger will soon pep you up after a long tiring day.

Serves 4

12 oz (335 g) peeled prawns	1 tbsp sunflower oil
1 red pepper	2 tbsp soy sauce
1 medium onion or 8–10 spring onions	2 tbsp dry sherry
1 clove garlic	1 tsp cornflour
1 inch (2.5 cm) piece of fresh ginger	black pepper
	1 tbsp fresh chopped parsley

Defrost the prawns if you are using frozen ones and pat them dry, or the surplus water will spoil the sauce. Quarter the onion and the de-seeded red pepper and slice them, or cut the spring onions, into 2 inch (5 cm) pieces. Peel and chop the garlic, peel and finely chop the ginger. Measure out the soy sauce and the sherry into a teacup; chop the parsley.

Heat the oil in a wok or large frying pan until it is really hot. Add the onions, garlic and ginger and stir-fry over a high heat for about 1 minute. Add the red pepper and stir-fry for another minute, followed by the prawns, which just need to be tossed around for 30 seconds to absorb the flavours and heat through.

Pour in the soy sauce and the sherry, which will sizzle wonderfully. Dissolve the cornflour in 3 tbsp cold water and add to the pan: the sauce will thicken as it returns to the boil. Season with black pepper only (soy sauce already contains salt) and serve sprinkled with chopped parsley.

Noodles are a quick, filling accompaniment.

Squid in Black Bean Sauce

This is a Chinese dish cooked by the stir-fry method. The secret of it is to have everything prepared before you put the wok (or frying pan) over the heat and start cooking. Toss and stir the ingredients over a high heat and then bring the food to the table sizzling hot.

Ready-made black bean sauce can be bought in jars in many supermarkets, but is quite salty. I have therefore included only a little soy sauce, as this also contains salt, and used fish stock from the freezer to make up the required amount of liquid.

This recipe is sufficient for 4 people if you are serving no other dish except rice or noodles. If you decide to have two or more main dishes, in true Chinese style, it will feed 6.

2 lb (900 g) whole squid
2 tbsp sunflower oil
2 fresh chillies
1 inch (2.5 cm) piece fresh ginger
1 clove garlic
8 spring onions

1 green pepper
2 tbsp black bean sauce
4 tbsp dry sherry
2½ fl oz (75 ml) fish stock
1 tbsp soy sauce
1 heaped tsp cornflour (optional)

Clean the squid as shown on page 54, cut the bodies into rings and roughly chop the tentacles. Wearing rubber gloves or plastic freezer bags to protect your fingers from absorbing the chilli juice, de-seed and finely chop the chillies. Peel the garlic and put it ready in a garlic press. Peel and chop the ginger, slice the spring onions into ½ inch (1 cm) lengths and de-seed and slice the green pepper. Mix the fish stock, soy sauce, black bean sauce and sherry in a mug. Put everything to hand by the side of the stove. Put the noodles on to cook. (If you are serving rice, you will need to put it on to boil earlier.)

Heat the oil in a wok or large frying pan over a high heat. Add the ginger, garlic and chilli and cook for 2 minutes. Add the spring onions and green pepper and stir fry for a further 2 minutes. Pour in the mug of sauces followed by the squid. Cook for 30–60 seconds, until the squid has turned white and is beginning to curl. If you prefer a thicker sauce, stir in the cornflour, dissolved in 3 tbsp cold water, at this point. As it returns to the boil the sauce will thicken.

Serve immediately.

Fish Pie

This is a filling pie which costs very little to make, as it uses coley which is one of the cheapest filleted fish on sale. If coley is unavailable, use cod or haddock. If you want to be really economical, replace the prawns with frozen peas. With its rich shortcrust pastry topping, this dish needs to be served with nothing more than some fresh vegetables. For a variation of the same recipe, however, you can omit the pastry and cover the top with sliced tomato and breadcrumbs.

Serves 4

12 oz (335 g) coley fillets
½ pint (300 ml) fish stock
bayleaf
seasoning
1 oz (30 g) butter
1 tbsp white flour
¼ pint (150 ml) milk
pinch dry mustard

3 hard-boiled eggs
2 oz (55 g) peeled prawns
1 oz (30 g) grated Parmesan cheese
Pastry
6 oz (170 g) white flour
3 oz (85 g) butter or hard margarine
2 tbsp cold water
beaten egg for glazing

Skin the fish fillets and poach them in the stock with the bayleaf and some seasoning for 10 minutes on top of the stove. Remove them with a slotted spoon and cool. Strain the stock and keep it to one side for making the sauce. Make the pastry according to the method on page 190. Put it in the fridge to chill.

Melt the butter in a non-stick saucepan, add the flour and make a roux. Make the stock up to nearly ¾ pint (450 ml) with the milk and blend it into the roux, stirring till smooth. Add the mustard and cook gently over a low heat for 10 minutes, stirring occasionally. The sauce should not be too thick at this stage, or the later addition of the cheese and eggs will make it rather solid.

Remove any bones from the cooled fish and divide it into chunks. Stir these into the sauce with the chopped hard-boiled egg, cheese and prawns (thoroughly defrosted and dried if using frozen ones). Season and empty the whole lot into a medium-sized pie dish.

Roll out the pastry and cover the pie dish with it, cutting off any surplus round the sides and using this for decoration. Crimp the edges by pinching all round with your finger and thumb. (The whole dish can be prepared in advance to this stage.) Brush the pastry with the beaten egg and bake the pie in an oven preheated to Gas 6/400°F/200°C for 30–40 minutes until the pastry is golden brown and the filling bubbling hot.

Skate and Mushroom Pie

This pie is made in a small flan tin with a removable base. The filling is enclosed with shortcrust pastry. Since skate is a meaty fish you won't need to accompany this dish with much more than a simply cooked vegetable like broccoli or beans. Try and use the larger flat mushrooms for the sauce, rather than the button variety, as they are much tastier.

Serves 3–4

1½ lb (670 g) skate
¼ pint (150 ml) dry white wine
¾ pint (425 ml) water
black peppercorns
bayleaf
few slices onion
1 oz (30 g) butter
4 oz (110 g) flat mushrooms
¼ onion

1 tbsp wholemeal flour
seasoning
dash Worcestershire sauce
beaten egg

Pastry
8 oz (225 g) white flour
4 oz (110 g) butter or margarine
2–3 tbsp cold water

Bring the wine, water, onion slices, peppercorns and bayleaf to the boil and simmer covered for 15 minutes to make a court bouillon. Strain and cool slightly.

Put the piece of skate in a roasting tin or large pan and pour on the court bouillon. Bring to just under the boil and poach gently for 20 minutes. Lift out the skate, remove the skin and scrape the flesh off the bones. Put the bones into a saucepan with the poaching liquor and simmer for 15 minutes until reduced to ½ pint (300 ml). Strain and set to one side.

Make the shortcrust pastry in a food processor or by hand. Roll it out and line a greased flan tin, about 7–8 inches (18–20 cm) diameter. Roughly chop the cooked skate and scatter it in the pastry case. Chill.

Melt the butter in a pan and sauté the chopped onion and sliced mushrooms. Add the flour to absorb the fat and stir in enough of the poaching liquor to make a thick sauce. Season and add a dash of Worcestershire sauce. Set to one side to cool slightly.

Preheat the oven to Gas 7/425°F/220°C. Roll out the remaining pastry to make a lid for the pie. Pour the mushroom sauce over the fish and fit on the lid, sealing the join by pressing down with your forefinger all the way round. Make a small hole in the centre to allow the steam to escape, decorate with pastry leaves and brush with beaten egg. Bake for 25–30 minutes in the oven until the pastry is golden brown.

Remove from the flan tin to serve, but keep the pie on the metal base.

Prawn and Sherry Turnovers

Frozen prawns often don't taste of much, but here is a way to liven them up with the addition of dry sherry, which when used with discretion can make a simple dish taste really special. The puff pastry enclosing the prawns makes the shellfish stretch a long way. You will find that you don't need to serve potatoes or rice as well, unless you have really big eaters in the house. A good salad or some fresh vegetables to accompany the main course should be ample.

Serves 4

8 oz (225 g) peeled prawns	2 tbsp milk
6 oz (170 g) button mushrooms	black pepper
1 medium onion	1 tbsp fresh chopped parsley
1 clove garlic	1 egg
½ oz (15 g) butter	12–13 oz (335–365 g) frozen or
1 dsp wholemeal flour	readymade puff pastry
3 tbsp dry sherry	

If you are using frozen pastry, defrost it. Slice the mushrooms and chop the onion. Should your prawns be frozen ones, defrost them completely and pat dry with kitchen paper.

Melt the butter in a non-stick saucepan and soften the onion with the crushed garlic. Add the sliced mushrooms and cook gently for about 5 minutes. Add the prawns and stir in the flour, turning the mixture carefully with a wooden spoon so as to keep the main ingredients whole. Stir in the sherry and milk and cook, stirring gently, until the liquid has all but evaporated. Season with black pepper and sprinkle with the parsley. Set aside to cool.

On a floured board, roll out the pastry fairly thinly into a square about 10 x 10 inches (25 x 25 cm) or a little larger. Using a sharp knife divide the pastry into 4 pieces, each 5–6 inches (13–15 cm) square. Imagine a line drawn diagonally across each one. Cover one half with some of the prawn mixture, brush round the edge of the square with water and then fold over diagonally to form a triangular parcel. Crimp the edges together by pressing down with your forefinger. Repeat the procedure with the other three and brush each one with beaten egg.

Put the turnovers on a non-stick or greased baking tray and bake for 15–20 minutes in an oven preheated to Gas 7/425°F/220°C until the pastry is golden brown.

Fresh Prawns au Gratin

Good fishmongers often have two sorts of unpeeled cooked prawns on sale. Go for the larger ones for this dish. They cost about 25 per cent more than the smaller ones, but take less time to shell and have a firmer texture and better taste than the tiddlers.

This dish is quick to prepare and can be served as a starter by itself, or as a main course with vegetables and rice or potatoes. You could include a little leftover cooked fish if you want to make it stretch further.

Serves 4

1½ lb (670 g) unpeeled prawns
1 pint (550 ml) milk
½ wineglass dry vermouth
black pepper
bayleaf
parsley stalks

½ medium onion
1 clove garlic
2 oz (55 g) butter
2 tbsp wholemeal flour
3 oz (85 g) Cheddar cheese

Peel the prawns and put the shells into a saucepan with the heads and tails. Pour in the milk and vermouth and add the bayleaf, some crushed black peppercorns and the parsley. Bring to the boil, turn down the heat and simmer uncovered for 5–10 minutes. Strain the stock and set aside.

Chop the onion and sauté it with the crushed garlic in the butter until soft. Stir in the flour and gradually pour on the strained milk, which will now be well flavoured by the prawn shells. Stir continually to avoid lumps forming, then cook over a very low heat until really thick and smooth. This is a sauce to coat the prawns, rather than to pour over them.

Put the prawns in 4 well-scrubbed scallop shells or a small gratin dish. Spoon the sauce over the top. Grate the cheese finely and sprinkle it all over. (The dish can be prepared in advance up to this point.) Pop under a hot grill until the cheese has browned, and serve.

Prawn and Black Olive Pizza

Many people never make pizza at home because they are not confident about working with yeast, a vital ingredient in a true pizza dough to give that bready texture. Since the dough has to be left to rise for up to 2 hours as well, it is hardly the ideal meal, you may think, for those who are short of time either. However, if you use scone dough, which requires no yeast, you can make the whole thing in minutes. The resulting base is just as good, even if it's not completely authentic.

Serves 4

8 oz (225 g) peeled prawns
1 medium onion
1 large clove garlic
1 tbsp olive oil
1 tbsp wholemeal flour
14 oz (390 g) tin tomatoes
1 tbsp red wine
pinch thyme
pinch basil
seasoning

4 oz (110 g) black olives
4 oz (110 g) Mozzarella cheese

Dough
8 oz (225 g) white flour
3 level tsp baking powder
pinch salt
2 oz (55 g) butter
¼ pint (150 ml) milk

First make the topping by chopping the onion and softening it in the olive oil with the crushed garlic. Then stir in the tablespoon of flour to absorb the fat. Drain the tin of tomatoes, keeping the juice for some other dish, and add the tomatoes with the red wine and herbs. Season well and leave to simmer for 15 minutes, stirring occasionally.

If you have a food processor, fit the metal blade, sift the flour, baking powder and salt into the bowl, add the butter cut into pieces and switch on for a few seconds until the mixture resembles breadcrumbs. With the machine running, pour in the milk through the funnel in the lid until you have a soft dough. Remove it from the bowl, gather it up in your hand and knead once or twice. Otherwise make the dough by hand, first cutting and rubbing the fat into the dry ingredients, then adding the milk. The dough should be very soft and light. Gently roll it out into a large circle about ¼ inch (2 cm) thick.

Preheat the oven to Gas 7/425°F/220°C. Put the dough base on a greased baking tray and spread it with the tomato topping, which should be thick. Stone and halve the olives and scatter them over the top with the prawns, which should be thoroughly defrosted and dried if you are using frozen ones. Arrange the thinly sliced Mozzarella all over and cook at the top of the oven for 15 minutes.

If Mozzarella is unobtainable, you can use Cheddar, but don't expect the same gooey, elastic texture that Mozzarella gives.

Squid Pizza

An alternative topping for homemade pizza, popular with seafood enthusiasts, is squid, cut into rings. Follow the above recipe to make the scone-dough base and tomato sauce. Then take 1 lb (450 g) whole squid, clean them as described on page 54 and cut the bodies into rings. Leave the tentacles whole unless they are particularly large, in which case you should chop them.

Put the squid in a saucepan, pour over a glass of dry white wine and enough water to cover, add a bayleaf and some seasoning and bring to the boil. Simmer until the squid turns white (about 5 minutes) and drain. (You can keep the stock in the freezer to use in a soup.) Spread the pizza base with the tomato, scatter the squid all over and arrange the sliced Mozzarella on top. Bake in the oven as above, until the cheese is browned and bubbling hot.

Crab Pancakes

Here is a recipe which really makes a little go a long way. Cheap and filling, it can be prepared in advance and just heated up in a hot oven before serving.

Serves 4

4 oz (110 g) white crabmeat
2 oz (55 g) brown crabmeat
¼ onion
¼ pint (150 ml) milk
6 black peppercorns
bayleaf
1½ oz (45 g) butter
1 tbsp wholemeal flour
4 tbsp dry white wine

black pepper
4 oz (110 g) button mushrooms
3 oz (85 g) Cheddar cheese

Pancake batter
4 oz (110 g) white flour
pinch salt
12 fl.oz (375 ml) milk
1 tbsp sunflower oil

Make the batter by sifting the flour into a large mixing bowl with a pinch of salt. Make a well in the centre and drop in the egg. Using an electric beater or wooden spoon, mix the egg and flour together and gradually incorporate the milk, beating well all the time until you have a smooth batter. Leave to stand for 30 minutes to let the starch in the flour swell.

Meanwhile start on the filling. Slice the quarter onion and put it into a small saucepan with the bayleaf, crushed black peppercorns and milk. Bring gently to the boil. Once boiling point is reached, remove the pan from the heat and leave to one side for the milk to absorb the flavouring from the other ingredients. Melt 1 oz (30 g) butter in another saucepan and make a roux with the flour, then stir in the strained milk and the wine, until you have a smooth sauce. Season well with lots of black pepper and stir in the crabmeat. Chop the mushrooms finely, sauté them in the remaining ½ oz (15 g) of butter and add to the sauce. Set to one side.

Heat a 6 inch (15 cm) non-stick frying pan and swirl the oil round it. Pour the oil out on to a little saucer and put in a couple of tablespoons (or half a small soup ladle) of pancake batter. It should cover the bottom, if you tilt the pan until the batter runs round the edge, but still be fairly thin.

As the pancake cooks over a medium heat, gently lift the edges with a spatula to loosen it. After about 3 minutes turn it over using the spatula, or toss it if you are feeling confident! Cook the other side briefly and slide the pancake off on to a large plate. Repeat until you have used up all the batter. This should give 8 pancakes if you have made them nice and thin. You should swirl out the pan again with oil after every two or three. Stack the cooked pancakes on top of each other.

Arrange about 2 tablespoons of filling in a line slightly to one side of the middle of each pancake. Roll it up carefully, tucking in the ends, and lay it in a greased ovenproof dish, repeating the process until all the filling is used up. If you are making the dish in advance cover it with clingfilm at this stage and refrigerate.

To serve, preheat the oven to Gas 6/400°F/200°C. Sprinkle the pancakes with grated Cheddar and heat through in the oven. This will take about 20 minutes if the pancakes are in two layers, a little less if they are single-layered.

Serve with baked potatoes and a crisp salad.

Crab Mousse

Here is a good way to make crabmeat stretch to feed a number of people. The quantities below will do 4–5 as a main course and 6–7 as a starter. To make it go further still, add a couple of chopped hardboiled eggs. This mousse freezes well.

1 lb (450 g) crabmeat, half white, half brown
6 oz (170 g) Quark or similar soft cheese made from skimmed milk
¼ pint (150 ml) mayonnaise
1 tbsp lemon juice
1 tbsp white wine vinegar
2 tsp tomato purée
seasoning
0.4 oz (11 g) sachet gelatine
¼ pint (150 ml) cold water
½ cucumber

Mix the mayonnaise and soft cheese together with a fork and stir in the crab, lemon juice, tomato purée and vinegar. Season well. Put the water in a small saucepan and scatter the gelatine over the top. Leave to sponge for a little while, then warm gently over a very low heat until the gelatine dissolves. Pour it into the crab mixture and mix well.

Empty the mixture into a 1½ pint (850 ml) soufflé dish and refrigerate until set. To serve, turn the dish upside-down on to a plate and, holding the two together, give a couple of sideways shakes. It should come out quite easily. Decorate the top and round the bottom of the mousse with thinly sliced cucumber.

To freeze the mousse without losing the use of your soufflé dish, line the dish with oiled silver foil, then pour in the crab mixture and freeze. Once frozen, you should be able to remove the mousse in its silver foil. To defrost, tear off the foil and return the mousse to the dish to thaw, before turning out as before.

Crab Soufflé

Soufflés are surrounded by a mystique that is quite unjustified. This one is particularly easy to make and gives excellent results. In a perfect world it would feed 4 but in my experience people always come back for more, so reckon on its feeding only 2–3 unless you have lots of other dishes to satisfy appreciative appetites!

Serves 2–4
8 oz (225 g) white crabmeat
1 oz (30 g) butter
1 oz (30 g) white flour
8 fl.oz (220 ml) milk
1 oz (30 g) Parmesan cheese
2 dashes Tabasco sauce
seasoning
2 eggs + 2 extra egg whites

Make a white sauce by mixing the flour with the melted butter to form a roux and then stirring in the milk gradually until well blended. Add the crabmeat, cheese, Tabasco and seasoning and heat through gently.

Grease a 1¼ pint (600 ml) soufflé dish (size 5) and set the oven to Gas 5/375°F/190°C. Separate the eggs and whip the 4 egg whites until the peaks still just flop over when you lift out the whisk. If you whip them too stiffly it will be more difficult to fold them into the crab mixture. Stir

2 of the egg yolks into the crab sauce when it has cooled a little, then turn this into a large mixing bowl. (Keep the remaining yolks for glazing pastry, scrambled eggs etc.)

Add 1 tablespoon of egg white to the crab mixture and stir in with a metal spoon to lighten it slightly, then fold in the remaining egg whites with a wide spatula. Don't overwork it or all the air will go out of the whites — it doesn't matter if there is the odd streak of unblended egg white to be seen.

Turn the whole lot into the soufflé dish, it should come to within ½ inch (1.5 cm) of the top. Give the dish a couple of sharp raps on the work surface to settle the contents and bake in the middle of the preheated oven for 35 minutes.

Serve immediately.

Smoked Haddock and Spinach Roulade

Light, delicate and cheap to make, this is good for making a little stretch a long way. Those who have not previously attempted a roulade, a rolled-up soufflé which looks like a Swiss roll, should not be put off — it is easier to make than you may suppose. Follow the instructions carefully the first time and you'll soon get the hang of it. Choose haddock that contains no artificial dyes or preservatives.

Serves 4

12 oz (335 g) smoked haddock
½ pint (300 ml) milk
bayleaf
black peppercorns
¼ sliced onion
1 lb (450 g) fresh or 8 oz (225 g) frozen spinach

6 eggs
2½ fl.oz (75 ml) double cream
1 tbsp grated Parmesan cheese
1 oz (30 g) butter
1 oz (30 g) white flour

Wash the spinach really well if it is fresh, snap off the large stalks and put into a big pan with no added liquid to cook over a gentle heat, turning the spinach occasionally with a large spoon. This will take about 5 minutes. Drain and squeeze between two plates to remove all liquid. If you are using frozen spinach, defrost it in a saucepan over a gentle heat until all excess water has evaporated. Chop finely and set aside.

Skin the haddock and poach it for 10 minutes on top of the stove in a large pan containing the milk, bayleaf, some crushed black peppercorns and the sliced onion quarter. Put two of the eggs on to hard-boil and separate the remaining four into two large mixing bowls.

Remove the poached haddock and strain the milk into a jug. Purée the fish in a food processor or mash it very well indeed with a fork, then beat lightly into the egg yolks together with the cream and Parmesan. Whip the egg whites until stiff and fold them into the fish mixture. Grease a piece of greaseproof paper or silver foil and lay it on a baking sheet or Swiss roll tin, about 13 x 9 inches (33 x 23 cm). Pour the soufflé mixture evenly on to this and bake for 15 minutes at Gas 6/400°F/200°C, until firm and just turning golden.

While this is cooking, make a roux with the butter and flour and blend in the flavoured milk to make a thick béchamel sauce. Simmer for 5 or more minutes to cook the flour contained in it, then stir in the spinach and chopped hardboiled eggs. Keep warm.

Remove the cooked soufflé mixture from the oven, and carefully but quickly turn it on to a clean tea towel on the work surface. Peel off the paper or foil, spread with the hot spinach sauce and roll up from one shorter end to the other. You may find it easier to do this by lifting the nearest side of the tea towel away from the work surface and, holding the two corners, moving it away from you, keeping it just a few inches above the soufflé mixture, which will then roll up automatically.

Slide on to a warmed serving dish and serve immediately.

Smoked Haddock Lasagne

The advantages of lasagne from the cook's point of view are many: it is cheap, filling, popular with everyone from grandparents to children, can be prepared way in advance and even frozen. The disadvantage is that it is a bit fiddly to prepare: you have to make two different sauces, cook the fish, grate the cheese — sometimes you wonder how the array of bubbling pans is ever going to end up as a unified dish. Persevere and allow 45 minutes for preparation, the result is worth it! You could even buy double the quantities below and make an extra one to keep in the freezer (for up to 2 months).

Serves 6–8
2 lb (900 g) smoked haddock
1¼ pints (600 ml) milk
½ medium onion
2 bayleaves
2 tsp anchovy essence
1½ oz (45 g) butter
1½ oz (45 g) white flour
seasoning
3 oz (85 g) Cheddar cheese
at least 9 oz (250 g) dried lasagne

Tomato sauce
1 tbsp olive oil
1 medium onion
1 clove garlic
2 tbsp white flour
1 lb 12 oz (785 g) tin tomatoes
3 tbsp red wine
bayleaf
pinch basil
seasoning

Skin the haddock and poach it in the milk, with the half onion, sliced, and bayleaves at Gas 4/350°F/180°C for 15–20 minutes. Meanwhile, cook the lasagne for 5 minutes, drain, and keep the pieces in a bowl of cold water until needed to prevent sticking. Lift the fish out of the poaching liquid and flake it with a fork. Stir in the anchovy essence. Strain the milk and let it cool.

Melt the butter in a non-stick saucepan and make a roux with the flour. Gradually add the flavoured milk, stirring continually until smooth. Season well. Stir the fish into this béchamel sauce.

To make the tomato sauce, finely chop the onion and sauté it in the oil in a non-stick pan with the crushed garlic. Stir in the flour and add the tinned tomatoes, crushing them well with a potato masher. Add the wine, herbs and seasoning, and simmer for 20 minutes. This sauce should be pretty thick due to the flour, but will need stirring from time to time while cooking to prevent it sticking.

Grease a rectangular roasting tin or ovenproof dish about 8 x 10 inches (20 x 25 cms). Pat the lasagne pieces dry and cover the bottom with a third of them. Spoon over half the tomato sauce, cover with more lasagne, and spread half the fishy béchamel over this. Repeat, so the top layer is fish sauce again. Grate the cheese and sprinkle it all over the top.

The dish can be frozen or stored in the fridge at this point. Defrost thoroughly and return to room temperature before cooking for 45–60 minutes at Gas 5/375°F/190°C until the cheese is browned. If you are going straight ahead with cooking the dish once it is prepared, the layers will still be quite warm, in which case it only needs about 30 minutes at the same temperature.

Smoked Haddock Cannelloni

A very economical dish that can be made in advance as well as frozen once cooked. The cheese sauce goes very well with the smoked haddock and in many ways this is superior to cannelloni made with meat. Try to find smoked haddock with no artificial colouring or preservatives.

Serves 4

1 lb (450 g) smoked haddock
¼ pint (150 ml) milk
bayleaf
½ small onion
black peppercorns
1 hardboiled egg
seasoning
1 tbsp fresh chopped parsley
12 cannelloni shapes

Cheese sauce
2 oz (55 g) butter
2 oz (55 g) white flour
1¼ pints (600 ml) milk plus
   poaching liquor
4 oz (110 g) Cheddar

Skin the haddock and poach it in the milk, with the sliced onion, bayleaf and crushed peppercorns for 10 minutes. Remove the fish after this time and flake it well, picking out any stray bones you see. Strain the poaching liquor into a measuring jug.

Chop the hardboiled egg and mix it with the fish and parsley. Season with black pepper and set aside.

To make the cheese sauce, melt the butter in a non-stick pan and stir in the flour to make a roux. Make the milk in the jug up to 1½ pints (850 ml) and gradually add it to the roux, stirring continually. Grate the cheese and mix in three-quarters of it. The sauce should be thick, but still of a pouring consistency.

Stir 4 tbsp of the sauce into the fish mixture and then, using your fingers, stuff the cannelloni tubes with the fish. Pour half the remaining sauce over the bottom of an ovenproof dish, large enough to hold all the cannelloni in one layer. Lay them on top, pour over the rest of the sauce and sprinkle with the remaining cheese. Bake in a preheated oven for 40 minutes at Gas 6/400°F/200°C until the pasta has cooked and the top browned.

If freezing, defrost thoroughly, then reheat covered at the same oven temperature for 20 minutes.

Seafood Salad

I regard this as a very British salad, made entirely from seafood commonly found around our shores. By all means make it in advance, but it should be eaten on the same day as you buy the shellfish.

Serves 4
8 oz (225 g) squid
4 oz (110 g) shelled cockles
4 scallops
1 pint/1 lb (450 g) mussels
8 spring onions
1 carrot
4 tbsp dry white wine
¼ pint (150 ml) water

heart of 1 head celery

French dressing
1 tbsp sunflower oil
4 tbsp olive oil
2 tbsp lemon juice
2 tbsp fresh chopped parsley
black pepper

Clean the squid as described on page 54 and slice the bodies into rings. Chop the tentacles. Wash the cockles under cold running water to remove any grit. Remove the scallops from their shells and wash well, scrub the mussels thoroughly, discarding any that remain open when tapped.

Put the scallops in a saucepan with the white wine and water. Bring to the boil and simmer, covered, for 4–5 minutes until the scallops are cooked. Remove them with a slotted spoon. Add the prepared squid to the same pan and simmer until the squid turns white and starts to curl at the edges. Do not overcook it or it will become tough and rubbery.

Add the mussels (you may need to pour the liquid into a bigger pan), and simmer until the shells open, about 5 minutes. Throw out any that remain closed and, using a teaspoon, separate the orange flesh from the shell. Put all the seafood in a bowl and mix it with the French dressing.

Trim the spring onions and using a very sharp knife slice the stalks lengthways into fine ribbons, making sure they are still attached to the main part of the onion. You will end up with an effect like a fan — drop the onions into ice-cold water and within about 30 minutes they will have curled round on themselves, making a simple but very attractive garnish for the dish. Pare thin strips off the peeled carrot with a potato peeler and leave these in the water too. Slice the celery heart and add it to the seafood. Sprinkle the salad with the chopped parsley.

To serve, pile the salad on to a flat dish, arrange the spring onions round the edge and scatter the carrot strips over the top.

Escabeche of Fish with Arequipeña Sauce

This Peruvian cold fish dish dates back to the Conquistadors, who brought with them to South America the ancient custom of preserving fish in a mixture of vinegar and oil. The fish is first lightly fried and then soused in the remaining ingredients. It keeps well, which suits a country like Peru, where refrigerators are still a luxury item, and is often found as an hors d'oeuvre in the older-style cafés. Cod is a good fish to use over here, as it stays fairly firm and in one piece.

Traditionally escabeche is served plain, but I find the sauce given below from Arequipa — Peru's second largest city and a gastronomic centre — goes very well with it.

Serves 4

1¼ lb (550 g) cod fillet
salt
2–3 tbsp wholemeal flour
black pepper
4 tbsp sunflower oil
2 tbsp olive oil
2 medium onions
2 fresh chillies

1 large clove garlic
4–5 cloves
¼ tsp cinnamon
large pinch dried oregano
2 tbsp wine vinegar
2 heads maize (corn-on-the-cob)
4 oz (110 g) stuffed green olives
crisp lettuce leaves

Sauce

2 water biscuits or similar
2 oz (55 g) cottage cheese
1½ medium onions
1½ oz (45 g) shelled walnuts
1½ oz (45 g) shelled unsalted
  peanuts

1–2 fresh chillies
2 cloves garlic
2 tbsp olive oil
2½ fl.oz (75 ml) milk

Skin the cod fillet and cut it into four portions. Sprinkle liberally with salt and leave for an hour — this firms up the flesh. Rinse and dry the fish, then dredge each piece in flour, seasoned well with black pepper, shaking off any excess. Heat the sunflower oil in a frying pan and fry the fish until lightly browned, about 4 minutes on each side, depending on thickness. Don't overcook the fish or it will start to fall to bits. Remove the pieces to a deep china or glass bowl once they are cooked.

Without draining the frying pan, add the olive oil and stew the onions, sliced, the de-seeded and sliced chilli and the crushed garlic, together with the spices and herbs. When soft, pour this mixture over the fish. Swirl the vinegar round the frying pan and empty this into the glass bowl as well. Cool, cover with clingfilm and refrigerate for 12–24 hours.

To make the sauce, put all the ingredients except the milk in a food processor or liquidizer and process until really smooth. (Remember to halve and de-seed the chilli first.) Add the milk until the mixture is more of a purée. It should be thick enough to coat , but not thin enough to pour — like a mayonnaise.

Cover an oval platter with washed crisp lettuce leaves. Remove the fish from its bowl using a slotted spoon and pile it in the centre of the serving dish. Sprinkle with the sliced onions mixture. Cook the maize heads in boiling water for about 15–20 minutes until tender, drain and slice each one into 1½ inch (4 cm) wedges. Arrange these round the edge of the dish and scatter it with the olives. Serve with baked sweet potato and hand the Arequipeña sauce separately.

Smoked Trout Salad with Sesame Seed Dressing

Smoked trout is a delicious, delicate fish to serve with a crisp slightly bitter salad. Availability of the less common salad ingredients like radicchio depends on where you live, but try and make sure you have at least three different ingredients apart from the orange. Curly endive, feuille de chêne (a greenish-purple type of lettuce) and other new varieties are appearing in more and more good supermarkets. Go for a contrast of colour as well as taste and texture for a really attractive effect.

Serves 4

4 smoked trout	**Dressing**
4–5 radicchio leaves or similar slightly bitter lettuce	4 tbsp olive oil
1 bunch watercress	1 small clove garlic
1 Little Gem lettuce or lettuce heart	2 tbsp sesame seeds
1 orange	grated rind and juice of 1 lemon
	seasoning

Lift the two fillets off each trout and set aside. Take a large attractive platter and arrange the Little Gem or lettuce heart leaves round the outside. Cut the stalks off the watercress and wash the leaves with the radicchio.

To segment the orange, cut the top and bottom off and then, using a sharp knife, remove the skin by standing the orange on one end and slicing down, following the shape of the fruit and cutting through so the edge of the juicy flesh is exposed (this means all the pith comes off too). Then, holding the orange in your hand, cut down between the membranes to remove each segment.

Mix the radicchio, watercress and halved orange segments and place in the centre of the serving dish. Arrange the trout fillets on top so they lie diagonally.

Just before serving, heat the oil in a small saucepan, add the crushed garlic and sesame seeds and sauté them for a minute. Add the lemon juice and grated lemon rind, season and pour the sizzling dressing over the salad. Serve immediately with new potatoes.

Kedgeree

This traditional English dish is often associated with Edwardian breakfasts, when the sideboard groaned with food: hot savoury dishes like this one, grills, even cold meats. In these days of more balanced lighter meals, kedgeree has disappeared from the breakfast table to reappear as a popular Sunday brunch or supper dish. If you use smoked haddock containing no artificial dye, the overall colour of the dish will not be as yellow as some people have come to expect. The taste is just as good, however, and the avoidance of unnecessary additives can only be praised.

Note Leftover fish and cooked rice are two notorious breeding-grounds for bacteria, so once you have made the kedgeree don't keep it hanging around at room temperature. If you do want to make it in advance to reheat, refrigerate as soon as it is cool and reheat for a good 15 minutes, covered, at Gas 6/400°F/200°C.

Serves 4

1 lb (450 g) smoked haddock	1 oz (30 g) butter
bayleaf	2 eggs
black peppercorns	4 tbsp fresh chopped parsley
parsley stalks	3 tbsp single cream
12 oz (335 g) easy-cook rice	black pepper
1 medium onion	

Skin the haddock and put it in a medium saucepan with the crushed peppercorns, parsley stalks, bayleaf and 1½ pints (850 ml) water. Poach for 10 minutes and strain, removing the fish and setting it to one side. Keep the cooking liquor.

Finely chop the onion and sauté it in the butter in a non-stick saucepan. Add the rice and stir over the heat until it turns translucent. Pour on the liquid the fish has cooked in, cover and simmer very gently for 15–20 minutes if you are using white rice (allow 25–30 minutes for brown) until all the liquid is absorbed. If you think the rice is nearly ready and there is still too much liquid, remove the lid, turn up the heat and boil rapidly so the water evaporates. Meanwhile hardboil and shell the eggs.

Flake the fish and mix it into the rice with the chopped hardboiled eggs and the parsley. Stir in the cream, season with black pepper and heat through thoroughly.

Seafood Risotto

Quick and simple to prepare, risotto is something many people hesitate to attempt as it appears to be shrouded in some kind of mystique. All you need to ensure a successful dish for this recipe is Italian risotto rice, rounder and shorter than the familiar long-grain, and a good fish stock, which you can take from the freezer. Shellfish stock is ideal. Add the seafood at the end of cooking, using cockles, flaked cooked fish, or even frozen prawns — there is no set rule.

Quantities are for a light main course, served with just a salad.

Serves 4

1 lb (450 g) risotto rice	1–1¼ pints (550–750 ml) fish stock
½ medium onion	seasoning
1 clove garlic	4 oz (110 g) prawns, cockles etc.
3 oz (85 g) butter	1 oz (30 g) grated Parmesan cheese
¼ pint (150 ml) dry white wine	

Finely chop the onion and sauté it in a heavy-bottomed pan with 1 oz (30 g) butter and the crushed garlic till a pale golden colour. Add the rice (which you should not wash) and stir for 3–4 minutes in the hot butter. Pour on 1 pint (550 ml) of the stock and the wine, continue stirring until it comes to the boil. Season lightly, put on the lid, which you should weight if it is not close-fitting, and leave undisturbed over a very gentle heat for 15 minutes.

After this time check to see if the stock has been absorbed. If most of the liquid has gone and the rice is not quite cooked, add a little more stock, which should be at boiling temperature to avoid arresting the cooking process.

The total cooking time will be about 20–25 minutes, depending on the brand of rice used and the thickness of your pan. For the last few minutes it is advisable to stir the risotto gently, to prevent it sticking. At the same time heat the seafood through in 1 oz (30 g) butter in a separate pan. Stir into the risotto with the remaining butter and the grated Parmesan.

Serve with a really good leaf salad, using ingredients like radicchio, watercress, Cos or Webb's lettuce, and lamb's lettuce (mâche) if you can find it.

SPLASHING OUT

Soups and Starters

Clam Chowder

This is one of America's best-known traditional dishes and now that the large hard-shelled (or round) clams are more common in British fishmongers too, it can be successfully re-created here. There are several varieties of clam chowder, Manhattan and Boston being just two. Some use ingredients like tomatoes, green peppers and other extras, but here is the recipe for the simplest kind, the New England clam chowder. It relies on just potatoes and onions to accompany the clams to make a chunky, thick broth. It may not look spectacular, but its popularity testifies to the delicious flavour!

Non meat-eaters can omit the bacon, but should consider replacing it with something like smoked mussels so as not to lose the smoky base of the chowder.

Serves 4

10 large hard, round-shelled clams
1½ pints (850 ml) water
3 rashers streaky bacon or 3½ oz (105 g) tin smoked mussels
½ oz (15 g) butter
1 medium onion
1 tbsp wholemeal flour
2 medium potatoes
bayleaf
black pepper
2 tbsp single cream
fresh chopped parsley
croutons

Follow the instructions for feeding and cleaning clams on page 43. Remember to allow enough time for them to plump up and expel any sand (about 2 hours) before you start to cook. Discard any that remain open when tapped on the side of the sink and scrub the rest really well.

Bring the water to the boil and drop in the clams. Boil fast until the shells open — this happens quite suddenly after about 10 minutes, sometimes less. Remove them from the cooking liquid, which you should strain (preferably through a double thickness of muslin to catch any sand) and reserve. Remove the clams from their shells, pull off any bits still containing sand and chop the flesh finely. It should amount to about 10 oz (280 g) of meat.

De-rind the bacon and chop it finely. Melt the butter in a saucepan and sauté the bacon until crisp. Remove it and sauté the onion, also finely chopped, with the clams for about 5 minutes. Stir in the flour to absorb the fat and then add the cooking liquid the clams were opened in. Peel and finely dice the potatoes and add these to the soup with a bayleaf or two. Bring to the boil, season with black pepper only and simmer for 10 minutes.

Remove the bayleaves, stir in the single cream and heat through without letting it boil. Return the chopped bacon to the pan and serve it sprinkled with chopped parsley and croutons.

Bouillabaisse

It is not really possible to re-create in England the authentic Marseilles bouillabaisse, but as more and more new types of fish appear in our shops, it is getting easier to approach a successful approximation. The secret lies in using at least four different kinds of fish. For this reason it is not really worth making for less than 6 people. If you are cooking for more than that, add another variety of fish rather than increasing the weight of the others. It is fairly filling — served with French bread and a couple of good salads, this would make a satisfactory weekend lunch. If you have it as a starter, follow with the lightest of main courses.

Serves 6

8 oz (225 g) monkfish or other firm white fish
8 oz (225 g) haddock or cod fillet
8 oz (225 g) lobster (or crawfish) tail meat, or other shellfish such as crab claw meat
8 oz (225 g) whiting fillet
2 large onions
4 cloves garlic
5 tbsp olive oil
bayleaf
pinch thyme
parsley stalks
strip of orange peel
14 oz (390 g) tin chopped tomatoes
2 pints (1.1 litres) fish or shellfish stock
2 tbsp fresh chopped parsley

Skin the fish, remove the cartilage from the monkfish and cut it all into pieces about 1½ inches (4 cm) square. Divide the fish into two piles, one for firm-textured varieties which will need longer cooking (monkfish, cod, shellfish meat, etc.) and the other for the softer-fleshed fish like whiting, haddock, sole, etc.

Slice the onions and lay them on the bottom of a large saucepan or flameproof casserole. Add the crushed garlic and herbs, the oil, orange peel and the firmer-fleshed fish. Roughly chop the tomatoes and put them into a separate saucepan with the stock. Bring this second pan to the boil and pour the contents over the onions and fish. Keep the heat high and return the soup to the boil, then cook for 5 minutes. It should bubble furiously, as this creates a kind of emulsion between the oil and the stock and thickens the soup.

Add the other fish, return to the boil and cook another 5 minutes. Serve sprinkled with chopped parsley and with a small bowl of rouille (see page 189) so people can drop a spoonful in the centre of their own bowl.

Brazilian Fish Soup

The original Brazilian recipe for this soup included rather more exotic ingredients than can easily be found in the British high street, such as sea urchins. This version works very well though, and the end result looks most attractive, with the blue-black of the mussel shells contrasting with the pale fish broth, speckled with the green and red of the peppers and the pink prawns. Definitely a dinner party dish to impress.

Serves 4

12 oz (335 g) white fish fillets, e.g. haddock, sole, bass, whiting	1 green pepper
9 oz (250 g) peeled prawns	1½ wineglasses dry white wine
1 pint or 1 lb (450 g) mussels	1½ pints (850 ml) fish stock
1 tbsp olive oil	salt
2 cloves garlic	pinch cayenne
4 medium onions	pinch dried marjoram
6 oz (170 g) tin red pimentos	1 small glass dry sherry
	1 tbsp fresh chopped parsley

Peel the onions and garlic and chop them finely. Heat the oil in a saucepan and cook them for 5–10 minutes until soft. Finely chop the green pepper and red pimento and stir them into the onion. Cook over a high heat for 1 minute, remove from the stove and add the skinned fish, cut into small chunks, and the prawns. Set aside.

Clean the mussels thoroughly, discarding any which remain open when tapped. Heat the white wine in a big saucepan, add the mussels, cover and cook over a medium heat, shaking occasionally until the shells

open (about 5 minutes). Throw away any that remain closed. Set aside
eight for decoration and shell the rest, adding them to the pan
containing the fish and vegetables.

Strain the mussel cooking liquor through a piece of muslin to filter out
any sand and add it to the soup. Pour in the stock, season with a little
salt and add the marjoram and cayenne. Bring to the boil, cover and
simmer for 15 minutes. Add the sherry and chopped parsley and serve
very hot, garnished with two of the reserved mussels per bowl.

Thai Prawn Soup

This is a soup for people who live near the right kind of shops, since you
really have to use the ingredients listed in the recipe to get the authentic
taste (and this is my simplified adaptation of a real Thai version, which
has three or four *really* exotic ingredients). Chinese supermarkets and
greengrocers are good sources for the lemon grass and coriander,
although I have found lemon grass in Safeway occasionally. Greek shops
also stock fresh coriander. Try and buy good-sized prawns, and use sole
bones or cod scraps for the stock. (Leftover lemon grass can be sliced,
blanched and frozen, well wrapped in clingfilm and silver foil.)

An excellent starter for people who like spicy food, this soup is light
on the stomach and easy to make.

Serves 4

1 lb (450 g) unpeeled prawns	**Stock**
2 sticks celery	1 lb (450 g) sole bones or cod scraps
4 small carrots	Top part of celery head, including
4 plump spring onions	leaves
3 chillies	1 small onion, including (clean) skin
2–3 tbsp fresh chopped coriander	bayleaf
juice of 1 lime	black peppercorns
	1 stick of lemon grass
	2 pints (1.1 litre) water

First shell the prawns and put the shells, heads and tails into a large pan
with the other ingredients for the stock. The top of the celery head
should be roughly chopped and the onion halved, but the skin left on to
provide colour (wash it if necessary). Cover the pan and bring to the
boil, then lower the heat and simmer for 25 minutes. Strain and test for
seasoning.

Wash the celery sticks and the carrots. Slice the celery very finely and
halve then thinly slice the carrots, keeping the two separate. Wash and
slice the spring onions, including quite a bit of the green stalks so long as

they have not wilted. Wearing rubber gloves to protect your fingers from the burning juice, de-seed and finely slice the chillies. Chop the coriander finely. All this can be done in advance.

To make the soup, add the celery and the chilli to the strained fish stock, return to the boil and simmer for 3 minutes. Then add the carrots and simmer a further 7 minutes, making 10 in all. Put in the spring onion and the shelled prawns, and simmer 2 minutes, add the coriander and lime juice and heat through. Serve.

Crab Soup

I have included this in the Splashing Out section as the preparation time may dissuade you from making it as an everyday dish. It is essential to buy a whole crab, rather than relying on frozen crabmeat, because the shell is needed to make the tasty stock which is the basis for this really delicious soup. Use a skewer and metal teaspoon handle for extracting all the flesh, which takes about 25 minutes. Make sure you spread newspaper on the table first, as it's a messy job. If you don't have proper shellfish crackers to break the claws, use nutcrackers.

If you buy a live crab, cook it in the usual way and then follow the recipe below.

Serves 4–6

A 1½ lb (670 g) cooked crab
1 medium onion
1 large clove garlic
1 oz (30 g) butter
3 medium tomatoes
2 tbsp sherry or brandy
2 tbsp single cream

1 heaped tsp cornflour
seasoning

Stock
bouquet garni
¼ pint (150 ml) dry white wine
½ medium onion
1½ pints (850 ml) water

Extract all the meat from the crab (see page 45) and put it in a small bowl. Put the shell in a large pan with all the debris from the cracked claws etc. Add the bouquet garni, white wine, the half onion and water. Bring to the boil, remove the scum with a slotted spoon and simmer covered for 30 minutes. Strain and keep the stock to one side.

Chop the whole onion and sauté it in the melted butter with the crushed garlic in a medium-sized saucepan for 5–10 minutes. Quarter the tomatoes and add them, stir well and cook for another 5 minutes over a gentle heat. Add the crab stock, bring to the boil and simmer, covered, for 15 minutes. Put in the crab meat, which should weigh about 8 oz (225 g). Don't worry if it is not exactly the right weight, although if you have quite a bit over it is worth freezing it to use in another dish. Simmer for 5 minutes and then liquidize.

Reheat the soup, add the sherry or brandy and cream. Mix the cornflour with about 3 tbsp cold water and pour into the soup. As it returns to the boil it will thicken slightly. Season and serve piping hot.

Smoked Trout Pâté with Smoked Salmon

Easy to make, particularly if you have a food processor, this is a real treat. Being fairly rich, it serves up to 6 as a starter. Buy good-quality trout with no preservatives.

Serves 5–6

2 whole smoked trout, weighing 7–8 oz (195–225 g) each
2 tsp creamed horseradish
1 tbsp lemon juice
black pepper

¼ pint (150 ml) whipping cream
3–4 oz (85–110 g) Scotch smoked salmon
1 lemon

Cut the heads and tails off the trout and gently remove the skin. Take the flesh off the bone and chop it finely in a food processor or by hand. Mix in the horseradish and lemon juice and season well with lots of black pepper. Whip the cream in a large bowl and fold in the trout mixture.

Oil a 1 pint (550 ml) soufflé dish and turn it upside-down so any excess oil drips out. Line it with smoked salmon, using pieces that are as large as possible, rather than lots of little scrappy bits. Fill with the mousse. Gently fold the very edges of the smoked salmon over the edge of the mousse, thereby loosening the whole thing away from the sides of the dish. This makes it easier to turn out later. Refrigerate.

To serve, turn the soufflé dish upside-down over a plate and, holding the two together, give a couple of sideways shakes. It should all come out in one piece. If it doesn't, don't worry, just reshape it and use the smoked salmon to hide the repairs.

Garnish with freshly cut lemon wedges and serve with wholemeal toast.

Smoked and Fresh Salmon Pâté

Smoked salmon is a deservedly popular luxury. To make it stretch further, use it with fresh salmon in this pâté. The smoked salmon taste is still distinctive, without being overwhelming (many people find plain smoked salmon pâté too rich) and what seems like an expensive dish, actually serves up to 8 people. It also freezes well, wrapped in silver foil.

Serves 6–8

8 oz (225 g) fresh salmon fillet or 10 oz (280 g) if on the bone
4 oz (110 g) smoked salmon bits
¼ pint (150 ml) dry white wine
1 tbsp fresh chopped tarragon or 1 tsp dried

1 dsp fresh chopped dill or ½ tsp dried
black pepper
1 small clove garlic
5 oz (140 g) unsalted butter
2 tbsp fresh chopped parsley

Cut the fresh salmon fillet in half (or use 2 salmon steaks). Put these in a saucepan, add the white wine, tarragon, dill and black pepper. Bring to the boil and simmer for 5–10 minutes. The centre of the salmon should be cooked, but only just, appearing rosy rather than pale pink. Take out the fish with a slotted spoon and remove any skin and bones. Reduce the cooking liquor to a few tablespoons by boiling fast and set aside.

Chop the fresh and smoked salmon finely. If you use a food processor, be careful not to over-purée it — the darker colour of the smoked salmon should still be visible. Season well with black pepper. Sauté the crushed garlic in a knob of butter, melt the rest of the butter in the same saucepan and beat it all into the salmon, together with the reduced cooking liquor and the chopped parsley.

Tip the pâté into a small soufflé dish or loaf tin and chill for 2 hours or more. Decorate with a twist of lemon and serve with wholemeal toast.

Crab and Papaya Pâté

Once you have extracted the meat from the crab, this is very simple to make. Papayas bought from supermarkets are usually underripe, so buy yours about 5–6 days in advance, or the flavour will not be developed enough. They are sometimes labelled paw-paw and in this country are the size of a large avocado pear. The pâté looks very appealing served in the crab shell — proving again that presentation is half the secret of good food.

Serves 4

A 1¼ lb (550 g) cooked crab
1 papaya
1 tbsp mayonnaise

squeeze lemon juice
pinch cayenne
few crisp lettuce leaves

Extract the meat from the crab in the usual way, separating the white from the brown. The brown is not required for this recipe so you should freeze it for use in a soup or richer-tasting pâté. The total white meat extracted should weigh about 4–6 oz (110–170 g).

With your thumbs push down on the inner part of the underside of the shell to widen the cavity — you will notice there is actually a natural line drawn there to guide you, and the shell will break off along this line. Scrape out the inside and scrub the shell well.

Peel the papaya and halve it. Scoop out the little black seeds and cut the papaya into chunks. Put these into a food processor and blend until smooth. Mix the papaya with the white crabmeat, a good squeeze of lemon juice and mayonnaise. Pile back into the shell and sprinkle a little cayenne in a band across the centre. Serve surrounded by shredded lettuce and with a basket of wholemeal toast.

Scallop and Hake Pâté

This is a mild fish pâté that is quick to make, but it does need a few hours in the fridge to firm it up before serving. Sole or even whiting fillets can be used in place of hake.

Serves 6

4 large scallops	4 tbsp double cream
8 oz (225 g) filleted hake	1 tbsp lemon juice
¼ pint (150 ml) dry white wine	seasoning
1 tbsp mayonnaise	

Remove the scallops from their shells, wash well and cut them in half. Skin the hake and dice it to the same size as the scallops. Bring the white wine to the boil and drop the pieces of seafood in. Poach gently for 3–4 minutes until they turn white.

Strain (you can keep the wine to use in a stock or soup), and process the fish with the cream, mayonnaise and lemon juice in a food processor or blender until smooth. Season well with lots of black pepper and a pinch of salt and empty into a small dish.

Chill for several hours before serving with wholemeal toast.

Quick-Fry Scallops with Ginger and Lime

Fast, simple and wonderfully fresh-tasting, this is a luxury starter that makes the most of the tenderness of scallops. Good-quality frozen scallops could be used. (As scallops near the end of their season the frozen ones are, depending on size, generally cheaper.) To make the dish look really pretty, serve individual portions in warmed scallop shells — ask your fishmonger for the rounded shells when you buy the scallops.

Serves 4
14 scallops
8 spring onions
1 inch (2.5 cm) piece fresh ginger
1 lime
1–2 oz (30–55 g) butter
seasoning

If using fresh scallops, detach them from their shell and wash well; if
frozen, allow them to defrost. Pat dry and slice in three horizontally.
Trim the root from the spring onions, and cut into 1 inch (2.5 cm)
pieces, including some of the green stalks. Peel and finely chop a piece of
fresh ginger about 1 inch (2.5 cm) long or more, depending on taste.
Using a potato peeler, pare four strips of rind from a lime, shred them
into matchsticks and blanch briefly in boiling water.

Sauté the spring onions with the ginger in the butter for a minute, add
the scallops and cook until the edges are just beginning to curl up. Pour
on the juice from the lime, heat through, season and serve in scrubbed
warmed scallop shells, sprinkled with the shredded lime rind.

Avocado with Cod's Roe Sauce

This makes a welcome change from the ubiquitous avocado with prawns,
and has the added advantage that you can prepare it in advance, since
the sauce prevents the avocado flesh from discolouring. Make sure you
choose ripe avocados (they should 'give' slightly when pressed), or buy
them a few days ahead and leave them to ripen in a brown paper bag in a
warm place.

Serves 4
4 small or 2 large avocados
4 oz (110 g) cod's roe
4 oz (110 g) Quark or other
    low-fat soft cheese
juice of ½ lemon
black pepper
2 tbsp double cream
¼ iceberg lettuce
pinch cayenne

Skin the cod's roe and leave it in a bowl covered with cold water for
about 30 minutes to soak away some of the saltiness. Drain in a small-
meshed sieve and leave for a few minutes over the bowl to let any
remaining water drip out.

Put the soft cheese and the cod's roe into a food processor and blend,
adding the lemon juice and lots of black pepper (or mash them by hand
in a bowl with a fork). Stir in the cream.

Halve the avocados, take out the stone and remove the flesh by
running the metal handle of a teaspoon between the skin and the flesh.
Cut it into chunks and mix it with the cod's roe sauce.

Serve piled on to shredded lettuce in small bowls or scallop shells.
Sprinkle a little cayenne over each one.

Mini Crab and Avocado Pasties

Using ready-made puff pastry cuts down considerably on the preparation time for these miniature pasties, filled with creamy crab and chunks of avocado. Serve two per person as a starter and garnish each plate with some slices of avocado, prepared at the last minute while you quickly bake the pasties.

Makes 8

2 small ripe, yet firm, avocados	1 tbsp dry sherry
1 oz (30 g) butter	squeeze lemon juice
4 oz (110 g) crabmeat, half	seasoning
brown, half white	1 tbsp fresh chopped parsley
1 dsp wholemeal flour	8 oz (225 g) ready-made puff pastry
3 tbsp single cream	beaten egg

Halve one of the avocados lengthways. Run the metal handle of a teaspoon round between the skin and the flesh of just one half. You will find by turning it over on to a board and pushing with your thumbs on the skin, the flesh will fall out in one piece. Dice it fairly small and brush the other half with lemon juice to prevent it discolouring. Leave the second avocado untouched for the moment.

In a non-stick saucepan melt the butter and gently cook the crabmeat with the diced avocado flesh, stirring it very carefully with a single chopstick or small wooden spoon to prevent the avocado from breaking up. After a couple of minutes stir in the flour to absorb the fat and then add the single cream, sherry and lemon juice. Season and cook for about 5 minutes over a low heat until it thickens. Take the pan off the heat, stir in the chopped parsley and cool.

On a floured board roll out the puff pastry into a rectangle 8 x 16 inches (20 x 40 cm). Roll away from you rather than backwards and forwards, as the latter method, though quicker, will stretch the pastry and not give such a light end-result. With a sharp knife divide the rectangle in two lengthways and then across into four, so you end up with eight pieces each 4 inches (10 cm) square.

In the centre of each square arrange a dessertspoon of the crab mixture in a line. Cut off the corners of the pastry and brush all round the edges with beaten egg. Bring two opposite sides together so they meet in the middle and pinch the edges well to seal. Continue pinching the edges together down over the 'shoulders' and then flatten the ends, as in a Cornish pasty. Cut off the extreme ends to make them look neater. Cut two slits in each side.

Repeat with the remaining seven squares, transferring each one to a non-stick baking tray as you finish it. Try and keep your fingers as dry and clean as possible throughout.

Preheat the oven to Gas 7/425°F/220°C. Brush each pasty with beaten egg and bake them for about 10 minutes until golden brown. While they are cooking, halve the other avocado and remove the flesh from the skin as described above. Slice all three halves thinly lengthways and arrange an equal number of slices on four plates in a fan. Remove the pasties from the oven and put two on each plate. Serve immediately.

You can prepare the pasties in advance, up to the final baking. Just cover them with non-PVC clingfilm and store in the fridge, then brush with beaten egg before popping them in the oven.

Oysters Casino

This recipe is particularly suitable for the knobbly Portugese oysters. They are cheaper than our native ones and usually have a deeper shell, which holds the stuffing better. I have given quantities for 2 people, since few of us can now afford to serve oysters when entertaining a crowd!

Serves 2

12 Portugese oysters	1 tbsp fresh chopped parsley
1 rasher back bacon	few drops Worcestershire sauce
½ oz (15 g) butter	squeeze lemon juice
¼ medium onion	1 dsp dry sherry
¼ red pepper	black pepper

Prepare and open the oysters in the usual way, leaving each one on a half shell. Finely chop the bacon and grill it until cooked but not crisp.

Finely chop the onion and red pepper and sweat them in the butter in a small saucepan until soft, about 5 minutes. Add the parsley, lemon juice, sherry and Worcestershire sauce and season with black pepper. (Since the oysters are already quite salty, no further salt should be required.)

Place the oysters in their half shells in a shallow dish which fits below the grill, either resting on the grill pan or not, depending on your cooker. Put a spoonful of the cooked mixture into each shell, on top of the oyster, and sprinkle with pieces of bacon.

Grill for 3 minutes and serve immediately with brown bread and butter.

Oysters Rockefeller

Even the name of this dish smacks of the high life. It is said to have been invented in the kitchens of a famous New Orleans restaurant at the turn of the century, but like all celebrated dishes, there exist numerous subtle variations on the original theme. Here is one of them.

Serves 2

12 Portugese oysters	1 tbsp fresh chopped parsley
1 oz (30 g) butter	pinch cayenne
2 rashers back bacon	1–2 tbsp dried wholemeal
3 oz (85 g) cooked puréed spinach	breadcrumbs
(about 6 oz/170 g raw)	few drops Pernod or Ricard
1 tbsp finely chopped onion	

Prepare and open the oysters in the usual way, leaving each one on a half shell. Finely chop the bacon, cook and purée the spinach, or defrost it if using frozen.

Melt the butter in a small saucepan and add the chopped onion and bacon. Cook gently for about 5 minutes, then add the puréed spinach, allowing any excess water to evaporate by shaking over a high heat. Stir in the breadcrumbs, parsley and cayenne and add a few drops of Pernod or Ricard — I mean really a few, about half a teaspoon, or the strong aniseed taste will overwhelm the dish.

Traditionally this dish is served in a bed of rock salt, but a simple shallow dish will do. Arrange the oysters in the serving dish, with or without the rock salt, and put a spoonful of the mixture on top of each oyster. Bake in a preheated oven for about 10 minutes at Gas 9/475°F/240°C until they are bubbling hot. Serve immediately.

Cebiche

This is an unusual and unforgettable way of preparing firm-fleshed fish. It comes from Peru, which is the original home of so many vegetables we now take for granted, introduced to Europe by the Spanish conquistadors — potatoes, beans, maize, tomatoes, as well as chillies and limes, both of which are staple ingredients in Peruvian cuisine.

Here the fish is marinaded in lime juice until it is 'cooked', flavoured with chilli and garnished with another Peruvian fruit, avocado. After the spicy flavours your mouth is soothed with slices of sweet potato. If maize is in season, garnish the finished dish with sliced cooked cobs for a really authentic touch. This quantity makes a filling starter or light lunch dish.

Use monkfish, halibut, turbot, sea bass or even mackerel — the flesh must be firm or the result will be mushy. The less hot, triangular chillies the size of little unopened fircones are preferable to the long thin fiery ones. If you can only find the latter, tread carefully! Chilli powder doesn't give the same effect in this dish, and lemon juice, although it still 'cooks' the fish by its acidity, fails to provide the same clean flavour as fresh lime juice.

Serves 4

12 oz (335 g) firm white fish	heart of a Cos lettuce
2 fresh chillies	1 small red pepper
8 spring onions or 1 medium onion	1 avocado
juice of 3 limes	2 tbsp fresh chopped parsley
2 sweet potatoes	2 heads maize (corn-on-the-cob)

Halve and de-seed the chillies, slice them finely. Protect your fingers from the juice by wearing rubber gloves or encasing your hands in a couple of plastic bags. Slice the onion or cut the spring onions into 1 inch (2.5 cm) lengths. Remove any bones from the fish and cut the flesh into 1 inch (2.5 cm) cubes. Put these in a glass or china bowl and pour the lime juice over them. Add the sliced chilli and spring onion. Turn the mixture several times with a spoon to ensure it is well coated, cover the bowl with clingfilm and leave it in the fridge for 6 hours. Turn it every so often, to ensure the fish 'cooks' all the way through — it will eventually turn completely opaque.

Peel, halve and boil the sweet potatoes — they should be tender after about 15 minutes. Drain and slice thickly. Taking the washed, crisp inner leaves of the Cos, tear them into pieces and use them to cover the bottom of an oval plate. De-seed and slice the red pepper. Halve the avocado, remove the stone and run the handle of a metal teaspoon down between the flesh and the skin. The flesh should now turn out quite easily. Dice it and mix with the fish and red pepper.

Using a slotted spoon, remove the fish mixture from its bowl and pile it in the centre of the plate. Surround it with the sliced sweet potato and sprinkle with chopped parsley.

If you are serving maize as well, boil it for 15–20 minutes in salted water until tender, then slice across with a sharp knife into 1½ inch (4 cm) pieces. These are best eaten in your fingers.

Scampi au Gratin

I once ate scampi on the Adriatic (where the best variety comes from), in a simple Yugoslavian restaurant where they were served in the shell in a sauce based on tomatoes and garlic. The result, though delicious, meant that in shelling the scampi I ended up with sauce running down my arms and dripping off my elbows. Here is an altogether less messy way to eat them, which still tastes just as good.

You will probably have to use ready-shelled frozen scampi, which is sadly the only kind widely available in England. These are usually Norwegian, rather than the superior Adriatic variety, and owing to the lack of regulations about their packing, contain a high proportion of ice, sometimes up to one-third, so allow for this when buying.

If you wish to serve this as a main course, increase the quantities by one-half. Instead of serving it in ramekins, you can omit the Parmesan and just dish it up over a bed of rice.

Serves 4

10–12 oz (280–335 g) peeled scampi (weighed after defrosting)	4 tbsp dry white wine
	pinch dried oregano
	pinch dried thyme
1 tbsp olive oil	bayleaf
3–4 cloves garlic	black pepper
½ medium onion	dash anchovy essence
½ red pepper	3 tbsp grated Parmesan cheese
6 ripe tomatoes	

Peel the tomatoes by dropping them into boiling water for the count of 10 and then into cold — the skins should slip off quite easily now. De-seed the red pepper and chop it with the onion. Chop the tomatoes.

Heat the oil in a saucepan and sauté the onion, red pepper and crushed garlic over a high heat for 5 minutes, stirring occasionally. Add the chopped tomatoes, wine and herbs and season with black pepper. Cover and simmer over a low heat for 20 minutes. Stir in the anchovy essence and the peeled scampi.

Simmer the scampi just long enough for them to cook, without toughening. Spoon them, with the sauce, into 4 individual ramekins or cocotte dishes. Sprinkle with the Parmesan cheese and brown under a hot grill.

If you wish to prepare this in advance, don't add the Parmesan until the final moments, then put the dishes into an oven preset to Gas 6/ 400°F/200°C, for 15 minutes until the cheese is beginning to brown.

Crab and Mango Mousse

Some people look dubious when this combination is recommended, but the two distinctive flavours do complement each other wonderfully. Very quick to prepare, this makes four generous portions.

Serves 4

2 ripe mangoes	pinch cayenne
12 oz (335 g) white crabmeat	0.4 oz (11 g) sachet of gelatine
4 tbsp double cream	1 tbsp lemon or lime juice

Peel the mangoes with a sharp knife and slice the flesh from the central core. Purée this in a liquidizer or food processor and mix with the crabmeat and double cream. Season with cayenne. Put the lemon or lime juice in a small saucepan and sprinkle the gelatine on top. Leave for the gelatine to absorb some of the liquid and then warm very gently over a very low heat until the gelatine is dissolved. Stir it into the crab mixture and spoon into individual glass dishes or a soufflé dish. Leave in the fridge to set.

Either serve in the glass bowls, or turn the soufflé dish upside-down on to a plate, hold the two together and shake sideways. The mousse should come out quite easily. Garnish with little sprigs of mint.

Cold Salmon Trout with Mossbank Mayonnaise (page 145)

Main Courses

Lobster with Devil Sauce (cold)

For most of us lobster, because of its high cost, is a real luxury. One eats it so rarely, it seems a pity to smother it in thick sauces and fancy garnishes. I prefer to serve it as plain as possible, since fresh lobster meat has a texture and taste unrivalled by any other shellfish. This devil sauce lifts the flavour without overwhelming it and does not hide the appearance either. Since most fishmongers sell lobsters ready boiled, this method of serving it is quick and easy to prepare, and can be done in advance.

Serves 4

2 x 1½ lb (670 g) cooked
   lobsters
Sauce
4 tbsp olive oil
1 tbsp Worcestershire sauce
1 dsp fresh lemon juice
1 tbsp tarragon vinegar
1 tsp creamed horseradish
black pepper
1 bunch watercress

Salad
8 oz (225 g) brown rice
3–4 strips lemon or lime rind
½ green pepper
½ red pepper
⅓ cucumber
French dressing (see page 188)
seasoning

Split and dress the cooked lobsters as described on page 48. Keep the small claws for decoration, after you have extracted the meat, except for the one nearest the head, which is rather unattractively hairy. Whisk the sauce ingredients until well emulsified.

Braised Sea Bass with Ginger (page 137) and Brazilian Fish Soup (page 115)

Boil the rice for 35–40 minutes until cooked. It should still have some 'bite' so check near the end of the cooking time to make sure you don't overdo it. Some strips of lemon or lime rind in the cooking water add a subtle flavour, well suited to something accompanying seafood. Drain and cool the rice, dice the peppers and the cucumber.

Mix these with the rice and enough French dressing to moisten without drowning the salad. Rice salads can taste a bit bland, so season well — the use of salt is quite justified here. Spread the rice over a large oval plate and arrange the dressed lobsters on top. Spoon the devil sauce into the lobster shells and garnish with the small claws. Wash the watercress and divide it into two or three little bunches before using it to decorate the dish.

Don't mix the salad together too far in advance, as the cucumber will make it rather soggy — about an hour is far enough ahead.

Crawfish Tails with Fresh Mango Sauce

Some years ago I spent ten days on a coral island off Belize in Central America. The only food available was langouste (crawfish or spiny lobster) and we had it for breakfast, lunch and supper until I thought I would never be able to face it again. However, several years later, I can now eat it with renewed enthusiasm, albeit having sometimes to rely on frozen crawfish tails, its most usual form in Britain. Combined with this simple sauce I find they make a quick and easy dish to impress guests, while recapturing those exotic days on that coral reef.

Serves 4

4 raw crawfish tails, about 10 oz
  (280 g) each with shell
water to cover
1 glass dry white wine
2 bayleaves
black peppercorns

1 ripe mango
1 small tub (150 g) natural yoghurt
1 tbsp double cream
heart of a Cos lettuce
pinch cayenne

Defrost the crawfish tails. Bring a glass of wine with about 2 pints water to the boil in a large pan, add the bayleaves and crushed black peppercorns. When boiling, drop the crawfish tails in and simmer until cooked, which will only take about 8–10 minutes — do not overcook or the meat will become tough. Remove from the cooking liquor and run under cold water till cool.

Peel the mango — a fairly good non-messy way to do this is impale its stalk-end on a fork and, holding it in the air above a plate to catch any juice, remove the peel in downward strips with a sharp little knife. Slice the flesh off the fibrous stone and purée with the natural yoghurt in a liquidizer or food processor, or chop and mix by hand. Stir in the double cream.

Cut the undershell off each crawfish tail with a pair of kitchen scissors or poultry shears and discard. Remove the flesh, with a small sharp knife, trying to keep it fairly whole. Slice it diagonally and return to the shell, turned so the pink rounded side is uppermost. Arrange the tails on a bed of Cos lettuce leaves taken from the heart and spoon over the mango yoghurt. Sprinkle each one with cayenne and serve with a new potato or rice salad.

Sole with Cucumber Sauce

The sauce which accompanies this poached sole is a variation on the classic hollandaise sauce. Don't be nervous of trying this supposedly difficult warm butter sauce — all you need is a pudding basin which fits over a small saucepan, a balloon whisk (although a wooden spoon will do) and a little patience. The chopped cucumber adds a subtle and delicate flavour. This recipe uses a whole egg instead of just egg yolks, which makes it less rich.

Serves 4

4 x 6 oz (170 g) fillets lemon sole	**Sauce**
¼ pint (150 ml) dry white wine	½ cucumber
bayleaf	3 oz (85 g) butter, cut into 3
slice lemon	1 egg and 1 egg yolk
black peppercorns	seasoning
	squeeze lemon juice
	3 tbsp tarragon vinegar

Skin the sole fillets, fold them into three to make a neat parcel and lay them in a shallow ovenproof dish. Heat the white wine until nearly boiling, pour it over the fish, add the bayleaf, lemon slice and black peppercorns and poach the fish for 10–15 minutes in an oven preheated to Gas 5/375°F/190°C.

While the fish is cooking prepare the sauce. Finely chop, but don't purée, the cucumber, either by hand or in a food processor. Keep the skin on so the sauce will be flecked with green. Drain the chopped flesh in a sieve and then dry on kitchen paper.

Make a hollandaise sauce by the method described on page 184, but using the quantities given here. When it has passed the test to show it is ready, check the seasoning, add a squeeze of lemon juice and the chopped cucumber. Leave it over the pan of hot water long enough to heat the cucumber through. (If making the sauce takes you longer than the time the fish takes to cook, remove the fillets from the poaching liquid and keep them warm on the serving dish.) Spoon the sauce over the fish.

Serve with rice and a fresh green vegetable like courgettes, mangetout or broccoli. The sauce will keep hot in a small Thermos flask for a couple of hours.

Orange Sole with Hollandaise Sauce

The classic sauces that are served with sole all too often mask or completely destroy the flavour of the fish. It is becoming more popular to serve sole and other delicately flavoured fish simply cooked and to hand the accompanying sauce separately.

Serves 4

4 large or 8 small fillets of sole
½ oz (15 g) butter
3 spring onions
juice of 2–3 oranges
up to ¼ pint (150 ml) dry white
   wine
2 tbsp lemon juice

bayleaf
black pepper
1 tbsp fresh chopped parsley or
   coriander
tiny pinch chilli powder
hollandaise sauce (see page 184)

Butter a shallow ovenproof dish. Skin the sole fillets, fold them into three to make neat parcels and place them in the dish. Slice the spring onions, including all the green stalk that hasn't withered, and scatter over the fish.

Squeeze 2–3 oranges, depending on juiciness (Valencia oranges are good for yielding juice) and pour all but 2 tbsp into a measuring jug. Make up to 8 fl.oz (250 ml) with white wine. Add the lemon juice and pour into a pan. Bring to just below poaching temperature and then pour round the fish. Place a bayleaf in the centre and sprinkle the fillets with the chopped herbs, chilli powder and freshly ground black pepper. Cook the fish in a preheated oven at Gas 5/375°F/190°C for 10–15 minutes until done.

While the fish is cooking, make the hollandaise sauce, adding the reserved 2 tbsp orange juice in place of the usual lemon juice. Dish up the fish and serve immediately, handing the sauce separately.

West Country Sole

Sole Véronique, made with a white wine and green grape sauce, is a classic French dish. This is a humbler, but equally good, English version, made with West country cider and apples.

Serves 4

4 large or 8 small sole fillets
½ pint (300 ml) dry cider
bayleaf
seasoning

1½ oz (45 g) butter
1 dsp white flour
1½ Cox apples
1 tbsp fresh chopped parsley

Skin the sole fillets, fold the ends in to form a parcel and put them in a fairly shallow ovenproof dish. Heat the cider, add the bayleaf and seasoning, pour it over the fish and bake in an oven preheated to Gas 5/ 375°F/190°C for 10–15 minutes, until the sole is done. Meanwhile peel, quarter and slice the apples.

When the fish is ready, remove it to a warmed serving plate and keep hot. Make a roux with ½ oz (15 g) of the butter and the flour and gradually blend in the cooking liquor, with the bayleaf removed, to make a smooth sauce. At the same time, melt the rest of the butter in a small frying pan and fry the apple slices till golden brown.

Pour the sauce over the fish and garnish the dish with the apple. Sprinkle with chopped parsley and serve.

Sole with Shrimp Sauce

It is worth taking the time required to make the sauce in this recipe to obtain the delicate end-result. In other words you have to peel each shrimp — rope in some help and it won't take as long as you'd think, maybe 15 minutes. The only way round is to buy ready-peeled shrimps and use a shellfish stock from the freezer — the result won't be as good. However, the preparation can be done well ahead of the meal.

Remember to ask the fishmonger for the sole bones after filleting.

Serves 4

8 small fillets sole
½ pint/6 oz (170 g) unpeeled
   shrimps
¾ pint (425 ml) water
bayleaf
few slices onion

black peppercorns
1 glass dry white wine
1 heaped tbsp cornflour
seasoning
squeeze lemon juice
1–2 tbsp single cream (optional)

Skin the sole fillets, fold them into neat parcels and place in a flameproof dish. Return to the fridge until ready to cook.

Peel the shrimps, return the bodies to the fridge and put all the shells into a small saucepan. Cover the shells with the water and add the bayleaf, onion, and crushed black peppercorns. Bring to the boil and simmer, covered, for 20 minutes. Strain the stock into a jug and cool. The shells will have coloured the liquid a dark pinkish brown. All this can be done in advance.

Pour the stock over the fish fillets, add the wine and bring to poaching temperature on top of the stove. Poach gently for 8 minutes, then remove the fillets carefully and keep them warm on a serving dish.

Mix the cornflour with 2–3 tbsp cold water and add to the hot cooking liquor with the peeled shrimps. Bring to the boil and simmer a minute or so until the sauce has thickened. If you wish you may add a tablespoon of cream. Test for seasoning, squeeze a little lemon juice into the sauce and pour it over the fish.

Fresh Tuna with Sour Cream and Mushrooms

It is rare to find fresh tuna in British fishmongers and then it is pretty expensive, but for those who like a meaty, filling fish dish it is always popular. Here it is cooked in the manner of a Hungarian goulash.

Serves 4

1¼–1½ lb (550–670 g) fresh tuna (about 2 complete thick slices)
1 oz (30 g) butter
1 tbsp sunflower oil
8 oz (225 g) button mushrooms
1 medium onion
2 heaped tsp paprika
1 tbsp wholemeal flour

¼ pint (150 ml) dry white wine
½pint (300 ml) fish stock
bayleaf
seasoning
6 tbsp sour cream (less than ¼ pint/75 ml)
2 tbsp fresh chopped parsley

Cut each slice of tuna into two so you have 4 portions. Wipe the mushrooms and halve them. Slice the onion finely.

Heat the butter and oil in a flameproof casserole dish and sauté the tuna pieces until just brown on both sides. Remove with a fish slice and put on one side. Add the onion to the pan, sauté for a couple of minutes, add the mushrooms and continue to cook until soft. Carefully stir in the paprika and flour to absorb the fat, and continue cooking for a minute.

Slowly pour on the stock and wine, stirring continuously to prevent lumps forming. When smooth, return the fish to the casserole, add the bayleaf and seasoning if required. Bring to a slow simmer, cover and cook over a gentle heat for 15 minutes.

After this time remove the bayleaf. Spoon the sour cream into a small mixing bowl and add a couple of soup-ladles of the hot sauce little by little, stirring well. Return this blended mixture to the dish and gently stir it in (this is to prevent the sour cream curdling on contact with the hot liquid).

Sprinkle with chopped parsley and serve on brown rice.

Bream with Satarash

The soil of the valleys around the medieval mountain town of Mostar in Yugoslavia is rich and fertile and supports heavy crops of tomatoes, sweet peppers, cucumbers, onions and also peaches. Satarash can best be described as a kind of Yugoslavian version of ratatouille, though with a lighter taste and with the addition of rice. I was served this dish several times when staying with Yugoslavian friends and thought at the time what an excellent flavour it would give a firm-fleshed fish like bream, if cooked together. Here is the result.

Choose a 2 lb (900 g) bream (ungutted weight) which will serve four people. If you can find the sweet Spanish onions with the reddish flesh, so much the better, although ordinary ones will do.

Serves 4

2 lb (900 g) bream
2 tbsp sunflower oil
3 medium onions
1½ lb (670 g) ripe tomatoes
3 small green peppers

6 oz (170 g) risotto or long-grain rice
seasoning
2 tbsp fresh chopped parsley
3 cloves garlic

Skin the tomatoes by dipping them in boiling water for the slow count of 10 and then into cold — you will find the skin slips off quite easily now. Chop them roughly. De-seed and chop the green peppers and chop the onions. Do not chop anything too finely or it will end up as a mush.

Heat the oil in a large casserole (large enough to hold the bream) and sauté the peppers and onion for 5 minutes. Add the tomatoes and simmer, covered for 20 minutes.

Meanwhile gut and scale the bream and cut the sharp fins off. If your casserole is not big enough, you could cut off the head of the fish, or alternatively transfer the satarash to a thick-bottomed roasting tin and when the fish has been added, cover it tightly with silver foil.

Stir the rice into the satarash, which should still be quite watery, and lay the bream on top. Spoon a little over the top of the fish, but take care that all the rice grains stay immersed in the sauce, or they will not cook properly. Cover and simmer gently for 20 minutes on top of the stove until the fish flesh flakes off the bone.

Season, sprinkle with the chopped parsley and finely chopped garlic and serve.

Grilled Snapper with Apricots

Fresh apricots only should be used for this dish. Snapper is imported frozen into Britain and occasionally you will get one where the taste seems a little tired — the strong apricot sauce soon peps it up.

Serves 4

4 small snapper, 8 oz (225 g) each   ½ tsp cinnamon
1 lb (450 g) ripe apricots   juice of ½ lemon
1 dsp brown muscovado sugar   black pepper
1 tbsp water   ½ oz (15 g) butter

Halve and stone the apricots and set 8 halves on one side. Put the rest, with the stones which give the sauce added flavour, into a small saucepan with the sugar, water, cinnamon and lemon juice. Stew over a low heat until the apricots are tender — this will take about 10 minutes.

Meanwhile scale the fish and trim the sharp fins. Make two diagonal slashes in each side and squeeze a little lemon juice into these. Grind some black pepper over the fish and preheat the grill.

Remove the stones from the apricot sauce and liquidize it. Return it to a very low heat and taste — you might want to add a little more sugar, but it shouldn't really need it.

Grill the snapper for 3–4 minutes on each side under a high heat. While they are cooking, quickly sauté the 8 apricot halves in a frying pan with the butter. Pour the hot sauce over the fish or hand it separately, and garnish with the apricots.

Snapper Casserole

From time to time you see a large snapper for sale at the fishmonger's, weighing anything from 1½ to 3 lb (670 g–1.35 kg). Although imported frozen, the flavour is quite good, the texture firm and the fish not too expensive. Get the fishmonger to scale and fillet it for you and try it casseroled with this slightly 'hot' sauce.

Serves 4

1¼–1½ lb (550–670 g) snapper   1 red pepper
  fillets   4 tomatoes
1 tbsp oil   1 tsp brown muscovado sugar
1 clove garlic   dash Tabasco sauce
1 medium onion   2 tbsp dry vermouth
1 stick celery   1 tbsp fresh chopped parsley

Fold the fish fillets and place them in a casserole dish. They don't need skinning, but check they have been thoroughly de-scaled.

Slice the onion and celery, and de-seed and slice the red pepper. Heat the oil in a saucepan and sauté the crushed garlic with the sliced vegetables for 5 minutes over a reasonably high heat. Chop the tomatoes and stir them in with the brown sugar, Tabasco and vermouth. Simmer gently until the mixture is beginning to turn mushy and then pour it over the fish.

Bake, covered, for 25 minutes in a preheated oven set to Gas 4/350°F/180°C and serve with rice.

Braised Sea Bass with Ginger

I find that the spiciness of fresh ginger goes very well with all kinds of fish. It is a combination popular in Chinese cooking and I have adapted the Chinese method of braising fish more to suit Western tastes and storecupboards. If you do not have a pan large enough to take the whole bass (remembering that a heavy roasting tin is a good substitute), cut the fish across into two or three — the pieces can easily be reassembled on the serving dish.

If you want to make this dish for just two or three people, bream can be used instead of bass, in which case reduce the braising time to 12–15 minutes, as a bream is not so thick.

Serves 6

2½ lb (1.1 kg) sea bass
2 inch (5 cm) piece fresh ginger
2 tbsp dry sherry
4 tbsp soy sauce
large pinch brown muscovado
  sugar

pinch salt
½ pint (300 ml) fish stock
4 tbsp sunflower oil
2 tsp cornflour
8 oz (225 g) carrots

Gut and scale the fish and cut three diagonal slashes in each side. Leave the head and tail on. Peel and slice the ginger and rub the fish with the slices, setting them to one side afterwards. In a small bowl mix the sherry, soy sauce, sugar and salt together. Put the stock in a saucepan over a low heat to warm up. Peel the carrots and cut them into batons about 2 inches (5 cm) long.

Heat the oil in a large casserole or roasting tin. When it is really hot take the fish by the head and tail and carefully lower it into the oil. Fry for 5 minutes, then turn the fish over with the help of a spatula or two large spoons and fry a further 5 minutes. Pour off the oil, spoon the sherry and soy sauce mixture over the fish. Put the carrot batons and ginger slices round the edge and pour the hot stock over. Lower the heat and cover the pan with a lid or double thickness of silver foil. Leave to braise for 15–20 minutes.

The fish is ready when the thickest part (just behind the head) is opaque white and flakes easily when scraped with a knife. Lift it out on to a warmed serving dish, using two spatulas or fish slices, and keep hot. Mix the cornflour with a little cold water and pour into the sauce. Return to a simmer and stir for a couple of minutes until the sauce has thickened. Pour over the fish and serve with brown rice.

Tarragon and Courgette Baked Turbot

Turbot is wildly expensive but if cooked with care is really excellent, both in taste and texture. Here it is treated with utmost simplicity in a recipe that takes about 5 minutes' preparation. If you like you can serve it with what is known as a Trianon hollandaise, which is the classic hollandaise with a spoonful of dry sherry beaten in at the last moment.

Serves 4

4 turbot fillets of 6–7 oz (170–195 g) each	black pepper
2 courgettes	2 tbsp lemon juice
3 tsp fresh chopped tarragon	hollandaise sauce (see page 184)
	1 tbsp dry sherry

Skin the fillets, fold them into three to make neat parcels and place them on individual pieces of silver foil, which you have previously greased fairly generously with butter. Grate the courgettes over the top and sprinkle with the chopped tarragon. Season with black pepper and sprinkle with the lemon juice, then fold the edges of the silver foil together to make an envelope.

Place the parcels on a baking tray and cook in an oven preheated to Gas 5/375°F/190°C for 15–20 minutes until done. Meanwhile make the hollandaise sauce in the usual way and beat in the sherry when the right consistency has been reached.

Serve with the sauce handed separately, accompanied by simply cooked vegetables like new potatoes and mangetout or baby carrots.

Turbot with Cheese Meringue

An excellent way to use up leftover turbot, indeed any white fish with a good taste, this dish also looks terrific when served. I like it so much I actually make it with fresh turbot if there are no leftovers, but it is worth buying a little extra turbot if you are serving it at a dinner party, so you can make this dish the next day as a treat for yourself.

Serves 2

10 oz (280 g) cooked turbot	seasoning
½ oz (15 g) butter	2 egg whites
½ oz (15 g) white flour	2 oz (55 g) finely grated cheese
¼ pint (150 ml) milk	

Cut the turbot into chunks. Set the oven to Gas 8/450°F/230°C. (If you are making it from fresh, first poach the fillets in ½ pint (300 ml) court bouillon for 10 minutes in an oven preheated to Gas 5/375°F/190°C then turn up the temperature setting.)

In a small saucepan make a roux with the butter and flour then gradually blend in the milk, season and simmer very gently for 5–10 minutes, stirring occasionally. The sauce should be really thick. Whip the egg whites stiffly and fold in the finely grated cheese. Stir the turbot into the white sauce, pile this on to two scrubbed scallop shells or individual little gratin dishes and spread with the cheese meringue.

Place the two dishes on a baking tray and cook in the oven for 10 minutes until the meringue is golden brown and the fish mixture bubbling. Serve immediately.

Halibut with Pimento Sauce

Halibut has an excellent taste and firm-textured flesh. It therefore benefits from the 'no-frills' approach — this simple bright red sauce complements it well.

Serves 4

4 x 6 oz (170 g) halibut steaks	1 small clove garlic
¾ pint (425 ml) court bouillon	2 tbsp dry white wine
2 x 6 oz (170 g) tins pimentos	2 tbsp single cream
1½ medium onion	seasoning
½ oz (15 g) butter	

Bring the court bouillon to just below simmering point. Place the steaks in a shallow ovenproof dish or roasting tin and pour the hot liquid over, then poach covered in the oven at Gas 4/350°F/180°C for 20 minutes, until the fish is done.

Meanwhile, make the sauce. Remove the pimentos from the tin, reserving the brine, and chop them roughly. Chop the onion and sweat it in the butter in a small saucepan with the crushed garlic and pimentos. After 10 minutes test for seasoning and stir in the wine and a couple of tablespoons of the brine. Liquidize the sauce until smooth.

Return it to the rinsed-out pan and stir in the cream. The finished sauce should be of a pouring consistency, but still quite thick. Remove the fish from the oven, quickly skin them and remove the central bone, as well as the small bones in the rounded end of each steak. Cover the bottom of four warmed plates with the red sauce and arrange the halibut steaks on top. Decorate with a small sprig of parsley or watercress and serve with rice.

Halibut with Dill and Lime

Halibut is a good meaty fish, usually sold in steaks, but it is also one of the more expensive varieties. However, you will find it quite rich and filling, so small portions are called for, especially when served with a sauce. One large steak can really serve 2 if you are having more than one course, but if you are big eaters buy one steak extra and share it between you. Halibut can be on the dry side, so it is better to poach it than subject it to the fierce heat of the grill.

Serves 4

4 small halibut steaks (6 oz/170 g) or 2 large ones (10–12 oz/ 280–335 g)
1 glass dry white wine
bayleaf
black peppercorns
slice lemon

Sauce
1 oz (30 g) butter
1 tbsp white flour
¼ pint (150 ml) fish stock
¼ pint (150 ml) milk
1 lime
2 tbsp fresh chopped dill

Put the wine, bayleaf, crushed peppercorns, slice of lemon and a little water into a shallow flameproof pan. Bring to the boil, lower the steaks into the liquid and poach gently until they are cooked, either in an oven preheated to Gas 5/375°F/190°C or on top of the stove. This will take about 10–15 minutes, depending on size.

While the fish is poaching start to make the sauce. Melt the butter in a small non-stick pan and add the flour, stirring to make a roux. Mix the fish stock and milk together and slowly add them to the roux, stirring well, until you have a smooth sauce. Lower the heat and simmer for about 5 minutes.

Remove the steaks from the poaching liquid and quickly take off the skin and central bone, as well as the small bones in the rounded end of each steak. Using a fish slice, put the four portions on to a warmed serving dish, cover and keep hot.

Add the cooking liquor to the sauce, stirring well. Grate the rind from the lime and add this, together with all the juice and half the chopped dill. Return the sauce to the boil, season and spoon it over the fish steaks. Sprinkle with the remaining dill and serve with steamed or boiled potatoes, or rice.

Salmon Steaks with Apple Brandy Sauce

A bottle of apple brandy, known as Calvados, is well worth keeping in the kitchen for cooking, since it goes so well with all sorts of dishes, particularly those involving apples, pork or chicken. Here it is used to flavour a sauce for salmon. Don't be tempted to use more than stated, or you will overwhelm the delicious flavour of the fish.

Serves 4

4 salmon steaks	2 dsp Calvados
½–¾ pint (300–425 ml) court bouillon	1 rounded tbsp fromage frais or 2 tbsp single cream
1 oz (30 g) butter	seasoning
1 tbsp white flour	1 tbsp fresh chopped parsley

Make the court bouillon in the usual way and strain it. Put the steaks into a shallow ovenproof dish and pour the liquid over. Poach for 15 minutes in an oven preheated to Gas 5/375°F/190°C.

In a small saucepan melt the butter and stir in the flour to make a roux. It should not be too stiff or the sauce will be too thick. Take the steaks out of the oven, carefully remove the outer skin and the central bone and keep hot on a serving dish.

Gradually add ½ pint (300 ml) of the cooking liquor to the roux, stirring well to avoid lumps. Stir the sauce over a low heat until it thickens, then season and add the Calvados. Put the fromage frais in a small bowl and whisk 2 tbsp of the sauce into it, then return this mixture to the pan. Whisk lightly until the two are well blended together and serve poured over the salmon, garnished with a sprinkling of chopped parsley.

Salmon Steaks with Raisin Sauce

Although a raisin sauce is traditionally served with dishes like tongue or pork, salmon actually goes rather well with dried fruit like raisins and dates, as you can also see in the recipe for Salmon en Croûte, Roman Style.

Serves 4

4 salmon steaks	1 oz (30 g) white flour
½–¾ pint (300–425 ml) court bouillon	4 oz (110 g) raisins
2 oz (55 g) butter	squeeze lemon juice
	seasoning

Put the salmon steaks into a shallow ovenproof dish. Heat the court bouillon, pour it round the fish and poach in a preheated oven at Gas 5/375°F/190°C for 15 minutes until cooked. Meanwhile make a roux with the butter and the flour and set aside.

When the steaks are done, place them on a warmed serving dish and keep hot. Blend enough of the cooking liquor into the roux to make a sauce of coating consistency. Add the raisins and cook over a fairly high heat for about 7 minutes, then remove from the heat, squeeze in some fresh lemon juice and season before pouring round the salmon steaks.

This goes well with puréed potatoes.

Summer Salmon Pie

Pie seems a rather plain word to describe this delicious blend of Scotch salmon and the first garden crops of the summer — young spinach and fresh mint. Topped with a light crisp crust of filo pastry it is a far cry from a traditional pie. Fromage frais is available in good supermarkets and delicatessens, but if you can't get it use low-fat soft cheese mixed with a little natural yoghurt.

Filo pastry, used for making strudel and Greek desserts like baklava, is also obtainable frozen from delicatessens. Defrost it under a damp cloth, unroll and use the sheets you require, then roll the rest up and refreeze.

Serves 6

1¼ lb (785 g) filleted salmon	black pepper
1 lb (450 g) fresh spinach	squeeze lemon juice
10 oz (280 g) fromage	approx 4 oz (110 g) filo pastry
frais (6 tbsp)	1½ oz (45 g) butter
2 tbsp fresh chopped mint	

The salmon should be in two or three large fillets. Place your hand on top of each one to hold it still and carefully slice it horizontally in half. Set aside.

Wash the spinach well and snap off the stalks. Cram it into a large pan without any additional water and cook until just beginning to soften, turning occasionally with a large spoon, then press between two thick plates to squeeze out all excess moisture. Put it into a food processor with the fromage frais and chopped mint and blend. (If doing this by hand, chop the spinach finely then mix in the other ingredients.)

Take an oval pie dish about 12 inches (30 cm) long and grease it lightly. Spread half the spinach mixture over the bottom, then put in a layer of salmon fillets, cutting them to fit if necessary. Spread these with another layer of the spinach and top with the rest of the salmon.

Cut 8 pieces of filo pastry a tiny bit larger than the inside rim of the dish. Season the salmon with the lemon juice and some black pepper, carefully arrange one piece of filo pastry over the top and tuck it down the sides. Brush this with melted butter and repeat until you have used up all the pastry, brushing each one with butter before adding the next. This will ensure the layers stay separate when cooking. Brush the top of the final layer with butter and gently score a lattice pattern on it.

Preheat the oven to Gas 6/400°F/200°C and cook the dish for 35 minutes until the pastry is golden brown and the inside bubbling. If the pastry is browning too fast, cover it with a piece of silver foil. Serve with rice or new potatoes and a good salad.

Salmon en Croûte, Roman style

Enclosing a piece of finest Scotch salmon in a pastry crust before baking it ensures that the flesh remains moist and succulent. By sandwiching the two fillets with a well-flavoured paste, you will find the added ingredients permeate, without dominating, the entire dish. I have done this successfully with asparagus, but an excellent alternative is a combination of the spices and fruits used in ancient Rome. The Romans frequently cooked their fish with chopped dates, cumin, mustard and honey among a range of other ingredients. These give a traditional rich flavour to salmon which is worthy of a banquet.

Serves 6

2¼–2½ lb (1–1.1 kg) piece of Scotch salmon, not including the head

½ tsp Dijon mustard
1 dsp fresh chopped mint or 1 tsp dried
2 tbsp clear honey

Paste
4 oz (110 g) fresh dates
9 whole cloves
2 oz (55 g) butter
1 tbsp raisins
¼ tsp ground ginger
½ tsp cumin

Shortcrust pastry
8 oz (225 g) white flour
5 oz (140 g) butter or hard margarine
1 egg
2 tbsp cold water

Ask the fishmonger to fillet and skin the salmon. When you get it home check the inner side of the fillets for any bones left in and pull these out with a pair of tweezers — you don't want anything to mar the perfection of this dish. Make the shortcrust pastry (see page 190), either in a food processor or by hand.

Stone, peel and chop the dates. Pound the cloves to a powder either in a mortar and pestle or by wrapping them in the corner of a clean tea towel and beating with a rolling pin. Melt the butter and mix it into the dates, cloves and other paste ingredients, stirring in the honey at the end.

Take two-thirds of the spicy paste and spread it over the inside of one salmon fillet. Sandwich the second on top, inner side down but facing the other way, so you don't have the two thicker sides together which would make the parcel lop-sided. Spread the rest of the paste on top. Roll the pastry out, not too thinly or it will burst during cooking, into a rectangle about 16 x 12 inches (40 x 30 cm).

Holding the salmon firmly at both ends, turn it upside down on to the pastry and bring the edges up to form a parcel, wetting them where they overlap. Make sure the joins are well sealed by brushing them with water. Use the surplus scraps of pastry to make decorations in the form of leaves or little fish. Turn the salmon on to a piece of greased silver foil on a baking tray, so the join is underneath. Stick the decorations on top by brushing their undersides with water. Brush the whole thing with beaten egg and bake in an oven preheated to Gas 7/425°F/220°C for 30 minutes until the pastry is golden brown. Serve in slices.

If you prepare this in advance and refrigerate it, remember to remove it to room temperature about 45 minutes before cooking or the chilled fish will not cook through in the allotted oven time.

Ragoût of Salmon

You can quite often find the tailpiece of a salmon being sold cheaper than salmon steaks or the whole fish. Snap it up, for this part is the most moist and when made into a creamy ragoût like this will stretch to feed 3 or 4 people.

Serves 3–4

Salmon tailpiece, 1¼ lb (550 g)	6 oz (170 g) button mushrooms
2 tbsp dry white wine	1 oz (30 g) butter
bayleaf	½ pint (300 ml) béchamel sauce
3 slices lemon	2 tbsp fresh chopped parsley
seasoning	1 slice wholemeal bread

Place the piece of salmon in a sheet of buttered silver foil, wrap it up with a bayleaf, few slices of lemon and the white wine, seasoning well. Bake on a tray in a preheated oven at Gas 4/350°F/180°C for 15 minutes, open the foil envelope and leave to cool slightly.

Slice the button mushrooms and toss them in a pan in half the butter until they change colour and soften slightly. Set aside to cool. Make the bread into crumbs, in a food processor or by hand on a grater.

Make the béchamel sauce as directed on page 182. Skin and bone the salmon and break it into chunks (it doesn't matter if the centre is a little undercooked, as it has another period in the oven still to undergo). Put the fish in a small ovenproof dish with the chopped parsley. Test the sauce for seasoning and pour it over the fish, stirring to make sure all the salmon pieces are well coated.

Sprinkle the dish with the mushrooms and then top with the breadcrumbs. Dot with the rest of the butter. (The dish can be prepared in advance up to this point.)

Bake for 15–20 minutes at Gas 6/400°F/200°C until the top is browned and the fish heated through. Remember to allow a little extra time here if you have made the dish in advance and it is chilled from the fridge. Serve with rice.

Cold Salmon Trout with Mossbank Mayonnaise

I once had a job cooking for the Orient Express, when the summer lunch menu included salmon trout. Two of us cooked and dressed up to 23 salmon trout a day, yet I never tired of the finished dish: a whole succulent delicate-pink fish on a silver platter, simply garnished with thinly sliced cucumber and piped mayonnaise. It always looks impressive, is cheaper and often more moist than salmon and epitomizes the best of a summer buffet.

However, with the move away from elaborate cream-decorated desserts piping bags are nowadays rarely found in the average kitchen. I therefore tend to cover the belly-edge of the fish with sliced cucumber, and serve separately a runnier, less rich mayonnaise, known in our family as Mossbank Mayonnaise (recipe on page 187).

For 8 people, buy a 4 lb (1.8 kg) salmon trout, for 4 allow 2½–3 lb (1.1–1.35 kg), weighed with head, tail and guts.

1 whole salmon trout	1 glass dry white wine
2 tbsp sunflower oil	½ large cucumber
2 bayleaves	bunch watercress
black pepper	½ pint (300 ml) or more Mossbank
½ lemon	mayonnaise

Gut the fish and wash well under cold water. Cut a piece of foil longer than the fish and oil it well. Lay the fish on top and put the bayleaves and some lemon slices inside, with some freshly ground black pepper. Scatter some more lemon slices over the top, bring up the sides of the foil and pour the wine over. Seal the edges of the silver foil into an envelope and set the parcel on a large baking tray.

Bake in the oven preheated to Gas 4/350°F/180°C for about 40–50 minutes, allowing about 15 minutes to the pound weight. To test if it is cooked, open the foil and scrape a knife along the thickest part of the fish behind the gills. If the flesh underneath is pale pink, the fish is done; any signs of rosiness and you should give it a little longer.

Remove from the oven and open the foil to facilitate cooling. Leave on the tray until completely cold.

To dress, cut off the head and tail neatly. Turn the whole fish over on to the worksurface. This ensures that the rounded side will end up uppermost. Pull off the foil covering the fish and using a medium-sized knife carefully scrape off the exposed skin. Then cut along the middle of the fish lengthways down to the bone, and with your fingers spread to support its weight, move the fatter half on to a serving dish, turning it over at the same time to show the inner side. Move and turn the belly fillet to lie next to it. Since this is now the hidden side of the fish, the join will not be visible.

You can now lift the bone off the remaining half easily in one piece. Having picked out any stray bones, turn the fish over on to its prepared matching half, and remove any remaining foil. Scrape off the rest of the skin and wipe the dish with a clean damp cloth.

Thinly slice the cucumber, using a mandolin if you have one, and arrange it along the belly of the fish to hide the ragged edge. Wash the watercress, cut off the stalks, split the bunch into two and arrange at the head and tail of the fish. Hand the mayonnaise separately.

Fennel-Stuffed Brill

Here the fish is cooked whole with the fennel stuffed into a pocket made by taking out the central bone, and so looks particularly good when brought to the table. If you do not feel confident to remove the bone yourself, explain to your fishmonger what you need. The important thing is to keep the fish in one piece, even if it is slit down its length top and bottom. A good way to serve a small brill.

Serves 2–3

1¼–1½ lb (550–670 g) whole brill
8–10 oz (225–280 g) fennel bulb
½ oz (15 g) butter
1 large dsp fresh dill or 1 tsp dried
seasoning

1 dsp wholemeal flour
1 tbsp lemon juice
2 tbsp Pernod or Ricard
¼ pint (150 ml) fish stock
6 unpeeled cooked prawns

Fillet the fish, keeping it whole. If you find it too hard to do this from one side only (dark skin side), approach it from both sides. Trim the fins and tail.

Chop the fennel and sweat it in the butter for 10 minutes. Add the dill, season well and stir in the flour to make a paste. Pour in the lemon juice, Pernod and 3 tbsp of stock to obtain a moist, but not sloppy, stuffing. Put the filleted fish, dark-skinned side up, on to a large ovenproof serving dish. Fill the pocket in the middle of the fish with the stuffing, closing the slit when you have finished. Surround with the rest of the fish stock and cover with silver foil.

Bake in a preheated oven at Gas 4/350°F/180°C for 20 minutes, removing the foil for the last 5 minutes and basting the fish with the juices. Remove the dark skin and arrange the prawns down the centre of the fish, so their heads are sticking out from the stuffing.

Scallops with Broccoli and Mushrooms

Scallops are pretty expensive even in the height of their season. If you are serving this dish alone with rice or noodles you will need the stated twelve, but if it is part of a choice of main courses, Chinese-style, you can get away with reducing the quantities and thereby the expense!

Serves 4

12 scallops
1 lb (450 g) broccoli, untrimmed
6 oz (170 g) button mushrooms
1–2 fresh chillies, depending on 'hotness'
1 medium onion
1 oz (30 g) butter
1 clove garlic
1 small glass dry vermouth

Detach the scallops from their shells if fresh and wash under running water; defrost and pat dry if frozen. Trim the broccoli and wash the mushrooms, which you should halve if they are not bite-sized.

Cook the broccoli in boiling water for 10 minutes till cooked *al dente*. Drain and set aside. Slice the scallops round the waist into two or three, depending on thickness, using a sharp knife. De-seed and finely slice the chilli, protecting your hands with rubber gloves or plastic freezer bags. Quarter the onion and slice it.

Melt the butter in a frying pan and sauté the onion with the crushed garlic and chilli till soft. Add the mushrooms and cook, stirring, for 2–3 minutes. Add the scallops and sauté until they turn white, which takes about 2–3 minutes. Put in the cooked broccoli, turning well to ensure it heats right through. Pour in a small glass of dry vermouth. Return to the boil and season. Serve with rice or noodles.

Scallop Brochettes

One of the best ways to serve scallops is simply grilled on skewers, without any sauce to mask what is one of the finest-tasting shellfish. Frozen scallops can be used if no fresh are available.

Serves 4

8 large scallops
1 small green pepper
1 small red pepper
¼ medium onion

16 button mushrooms (about
  6 oz/170 g)
2 tbsp olive oil
4 tbsp lemon juice

Detach the scallops from their shells and wash well. Cut the coral off in one piece and slice the main body into two. De-seed the peppers and cut into 1 inch (2.5 cm) dice. Separate the different layers of the onion and cut these into similar sized dice. Wipe the mushrooms.

Put the diced vegetables and the mushrooms into a small pan with enough water to cover and bring to the boil. This softens them slightly and prevents them from splitting when threaded on to the skewers. Drain and put into a bowl with the scallops and their corals, oil and lemon juice. Season well with black pepper and leave to marinate for 30 minutes.

Thread the vegetables and scallops on to 4 skewers about 10 inches (25 cm) long. Preheat the grill and place the skewers under it. Cook for about 8 minutes, turning once and brushing the brochette with some of the marinade when you do so.

Serve with brown rice and a large salad.

Devilled Crab

Crab has a strong enough flavour to stand up to being devilled and this dish makes a good alternative to plain cold dressed crab. For a real feast, allow one small crab per person, although two medium ones should be sufficient for 4 people. Baked potatoes or rice plus a salad make this an easy meal to prepare in advance.

Serves 4

2 x 1½ lb (670 g) live crabs
1 tsp anchovy essence
1 tsp Worcestershire sauce
pinch cayenne
1 tsp strong English mustard
1 tbsp brandy

black pepper
1 oz (30 g) grated Parmesan cheese
2½ fl.oz (75 ml) double cream
2 oz (55 g) finely grated Cheddar
2 tbsp dried wholemeal breadcrumbs

Cook the crabs according to the instructions on page 44 and extract all the meat. Press down along the inside edges of the shell: it should break off along the visible line and leave a larger cavity. Wash the shell out well. Flake the white crabmeat and mix it with the brown, together with the anchovy essence, Worcestershire sauce, cayenne, mustard, brandy, black pepper and grated Parmesan. Whip and fold in the cream.

Pile the mixture back into the shells and top with the grated Cheddar and breadcrumbs. You can prepare up to this stage well in advance, but return the dish to room temperature before heating it up.

Preset the oven to Gas 6/400°F/200°C and heat the crabs on a baking tray for 10 minutes, until the cheese is melted and turning golden. Transfer to a serving dish, strewn with watercress or hot rice, and serve.

Seafood Paella

Ideally you need a proper flat-bottomed paellera to cook this in, but I have done it successfully, if less elegantly, in a shallow roasting tin. A 12-inch diameter frying pan with handles that can stand up to the oven is also suitable — the main thing is that the pan must be wide and shallow or the paella will turn out too mushy.

Use whatever shellfish are available at the time, but bear in mind the visual as well as the gastronomic effect. Always include one type of fish, like monkfish, as well as some squid. The shellfish could include mussels, prawns, crab claws, whole scampi or scampi tails, even small clams. Here I have used Guernsey crab claws, which are sold already prepared in packs of six or more, ready to eat and of good quality, and unshelled fresh prawns as large as I could get them.

Serves 6

8 oz (225 g) monkfish	1 green pepper
1 lb (450 g) whole squid	3 medium tomatoes
8 oz (225 g) unpeeled prawns	3 tbsp olive oil
1 packet Guernsey crab claws	2 large cloves garlic
1½ pints (850 ml) fish stock	pinch paprika
¼ tsp saffron strands	1 lb (450 g) long-grain rice
1 large onion	1 tbsp dry sherry (optional)
1 red pepper	

All the preparation for this dish can be done some time ahead. Peel the prawns, adding the heads, tails and shells to the fish stock. Boil up for 10–15 minutes and strain. Soak the saffron in a few tablespoons of the hot stock, this draws out the yellow pigment. (Always buy good-quality saffron from a reputable source, many poor varieties or even imitations are around.)

Remove the bone from the fish and cube it. (If you are using mussels, scrub them well, discarding any that remain open when tapped sharply.) Clean the squid in the usual way, chop the tentacles if large and slice the body into rings. Chop the onion, quarter and de-seed the peppers and then slice them. Peel the tomatoes by dropping them into boiling water for the count of 10 before immersing in cold water. The skins will come off easily now. Chop the tomatoes roughly.

Preheat the oven to Gas 4/350°F/180°C. Heat the oil in the paellera on top of the stove and add the crushed garlic and chopped onion. Fry them for a few minutes until beginning to soften, without browning too much. Add the sliced peppers and sauté another 2–3 minutes. Stir in the rice until it becomes translucent, then add the tomatoes, the saffron with its soaking liquid, a pinch of paprika and at least a pint (550 ml) of the stock. Bring to the boil and add the pieces of monkfish. Transfer uncovered to the oven.

Check on the paella after 10–15 minutes. If it has used up most of the liquid and the rice is not yet cooked, add a little more hot stock. At the same time gently fork in the squid. Scatter the prawns and crab claws (and closed mussels if you are using them) over the surface and sprinkle with the sherry. Return to the oven for another 10 minutes or until the squid are cooked and the rice, having absorbed all the liquid, is beginning to go crusty round the edges.

If you have used mussels, discard any which have not opened. Serve the paella immediately with a big salad.

Hot Speckled Fish Mousse

Cook this in a ring mould and the end-result looks spectacular — an easy way to impress dinner guests. Use a soufflé dish if you don't have a ring mould, in which case you should arrange the strips of sole round the bottom of the dish in a circle, with two strips meeting in the middle as a cross. A food processor or liquidizer is essential unless you want to spend hours chopping and sieving. The preparation may look rather long, but in fact is quick and can be done well in advance of the final cooking.

Serves 6

12 oz (335 g) whiting or haddock
  fillets
8 oz (225 g) lemon sole fillet
12 oz (335 g) fresh spinach
  (weighed before trimming)
3 oz (85 g) curd cheese
4 tbsp whipping cream

1 tbsp lemon juice
1½ tbsp fresh chopped chervil
1 tbsp fresh chopped parsley
3 eggs
seasoning
small knob butter

Snap off the stalks from the spinach and wash the leaves well. Put them straight into a large pan and cook over a fairly high heat, with no other liquid added, for 5 minutes, until tender and much reduced in volume. Drain and press the spinach well against the sides of a sieve or colander with a spoon or press between two plates, to squeeze out as much liquid as possible. Empty the spinach into a double thickness of kitchen paper and squeeze again.

Put the spinach into a food processor with the cream, cheese, eggs, lemon juice and herbs and process until you have a smooth purée. Season well and empty the purée into a mixing bowl. Skin the haddock or whiting fillets and add them to the food processor, chop finely and mix with the spinach purée.

Grease a 2 pint (1.1 litre) ring mould with the knob of butter. Skin the sole, cover it with a piece of wet greaseproof paper and flatten well by beating with a rolling pin. Cut the sole into 6 strips, each about ¾ x 7 inches (2 x 18 cm). Arrange them, equally spaced and skinned side up, in the ring mould, with the ends hanging slightly over the edges of the mould. Fill with the spinach and fish and fold the ends of the sole strips over the top. Pick up the dish and give it a couple of short sharp taps on the work surface, so the contents settle. Refrigerate until needed, but remove 45 minutes before cooking, to bring it back to room temperature.

The mousse is cooked in a bain marie. Put the filled mould in a large roasting tin or similar dish. Boil a kettle of water and pour it into the tin so that it comes half-way up the sides of the ring mould. Bake for 45 minutes in an oven preheated to Gas 6/400°F/200°C. When a knife inserted in the mousse comes out clean, the dish is ready. (If you are cooking it in a soufflé dish, it will take about an hour.) The mousse will stay hot for some time without harm if you turn off the oven and leave it in the bain marie.

Unmould the dish on to a serving plate and fill the centre with a bunch of washed watercress. Serve with watercress or hollandaise sauce (see pages 190 and 184).

Layered Mushroom Fish Mousse

It is important to have fresh herbs for this dish, as well as good-quality, unblemished pale button mushrooms. You can make it using just salmon, but for economy, half-salmon half-sole is excellent. If you are using just the one variety, you don't of course have to divide all the other ingredients into two to create the layers. The chopping can be done in seconds in a food processor.

Serves 4

8 oz (225 g) salmon steak or 6 oz
  (170 g) fillet
4 oz (110 g) sole fillet
4 oz (110 g) button mushrooms
3 oz (85 g) butter
½ medium onion
2 tbsp fresh chopped parsley

1 tbsp fresh chopped chervil or
  tarragon
1 large egg
5 tbsp dry white wine
1 dsp lemon juice
seasoning
a little sunflower oil

Finely chop the mushrooms and soften them in the butter, covered.
Finely chop the onion and add this to the saucepan, sweat for about 5
minutes over a gentle heat. Take the pan off the stove, cool slightly and
add the chopped herbs, beaten egg, white wine and lemon juice. Season
well.

Skin and finely chop the sole and put it in a small basin. Skin and
remove the bones from the salmon steak, using a sharp knife, or skin the
fillet. Chop the salmon finely, putting the pieces into a second basin.
Divide the mushroom mixture between the two, giving about two-thirds
to the sole and the rest to the salmon. Mix in thoroughly.

Oil a small soufflé dish or terrine of about ¾ pint (425 ml) capacity and
cover the bottom with half the sole mixture. Pack all the salmon on top
of this and finish off with the rest of the sole. Cover with a piece of oiled
silver foil and a lid, otherwise cover tightly with a double thickness of
foil. Bake for 1½ hours in a bain marie in the centre of the oven at Gas 3/
325°F/170°C. Cool and chill in the fridge, then turn out and decorate
with slices of cucumber or lemon.

Smoked Salmon and Avocado Flan

Smoked salmon scraps are often sold off cheaply in fishmongers and are
excellent for pâtés or, as in this case, flans.

Serves 3–4

4–5 oz (110–140 g) smoked
  salmon bits
1 avocado
8 oz (225 g) fromage frais
2 eggs
seasoning

Shortcrust pastry
6 oz (170 g) white flour
3 oz (85 g) butter or hard margarine
1–2 tbsp ice-cold water

Make the pastry in the usual way and chill for 30 minutes. Roll it out
and line a 7–8 inch (18–20 cm) flan case. Fill this with dried beans and
greaseproof paper and bake blind for 20 minutes at Gas 6/400°F/200°C.
Roll out the leftover pastry and cut out little fishes, marking on
an eye, fin, etc. with a sharp knife. Brush these with beaten egg and
bake for 10–15 minutes on a small baking tray.

Dice the smoked salmon (you may find some bits are too dry or stringy and should be discarded). Halve the avocado and run the metal handle of a teaspoon round between the skin and the flesh — you will now be able to turn out the flesh quite easily. Cube it.

Mix the smoked salmon with the fromage frais, the beaten eggs and some seasoning. Add the avocado and turn it gently until coated, being careful not to break up the flesh. Pour the filling into the partly baked flan case and bake at Gas 5/375°F/190°C for 45–55 minutes until the top is browned and the centre reasonably firm. About 10 minutes before the end of cooking time, decorate the top with the pastry fish. (If you put them on raw they would absorb moisture from the flan and fail to go the attractive golden brown which makes this flan look so pretty.)

ALL WASHED UP

Soups and Starters

Smoked Haddock Soup

A light soup where the distinctive flavours of celery and smoked haddock complement each other perfectly. It should be sieved to take out the stringy parts of the celery, or the result will be lumpy and unattractive.

Serves 4

8 oz (225 g) smoked haddock
1 oz (30 g) butter
6 sticks celery
1 onion
¾ pint (425 ml) fish stock

bayleaf
black pepper
¾ pint (425 ml) milk
1–2 tbsp fresh chopped parsley

Skin the haddock and dice it. Wash and slice the celery and chop the onion. Melt the butter in a saucepan and sweat the celery and onion together for 10 minutes, being careful not to let them brown. Add the fish stock and the bayleaf and season with black pepper — you probably won't need salt as the smokiness of the haddock will satisfy the taste buds sufficiently. Simmer, covered, for 10 minutes.

Add the diced haddock and the milk and simmer a further 10 minutes without the lid. Remove the bayleaf and liquidize the soup, then pass it through a sieve, pushing through as much of the bits as you can. You will be left with a fair amount of stringy celery which should be discarded.

Serve sprinkled with chopped parsley.

Tuna and Sweetcorn Bisque

This is a real storecupboard recipe for times when you can't get to the shops. However, you should still include fish stock (use some from the freezer) as this adds a definite fishy taste, without which the soup can be rather bland. It is fairly filling.

Serves 4

7 oz (195 g) tin tuna
6 oz (170 g) tin sweetcorn
½ oz (15 g) butter
1 clove garlic
½ medium onion
1 medium potato

1 tbsp white flour
¾ pint (425 ml) fish stock
½ pint (300 ml) milk
seasoning
1–2 tbsp fresh chopped parsley

Dice the onion and peeled potato and sauté them in the melted butter in a saucepan with the crushed garlic for 5 minutes. Stir in the flour, cook for a minute or two and then blend in the fish stock. Bring to the boil, season and simmer, covered, for 10–15 minutes. Don't add the milk yet, or you will find the pan boils over every time you put the lid on.

Flake the tuna well with a fork and add it to the soup with the drained sweetcorn and milk. Simmer gently for 5 minutes to blend the flavours and test for seasoning. Serve, sprinkled with chopped parsley and accompanied by a basket of wholemeal rolls or bread.

Smoked Haddock and Whisky Tartlets

You may think whisky is an odd beverage to use in cooking, but its smoky taste goes surprisingly well with smoked haddock. Serve these with drinks, or omit the pastry and cook the mixture in ramekins to make a hot starter.

Makes 12 tartlets/4 ramekins

12 oz (335 g) smoked haddock
½ pint (300 ml) milk
bayleaf
black peppercorns
4 oz (110 g) low-fat cream cheese
2 tbsp Scotch whisky
seasoning
2 oz (55 g) butter

Pastry
6 oz (170 g) white flour
3½ oz (100 g) hard margarine
1–2 tbsp cold water

Make the pastry in a food processor or by hand (see page 190). Roll it out and cut out 12 rounds using a 3½ inch (9 cm) diameter crinkled pastry cutter. Line a tray of straight-sided tartlet tins, each 2½ inches (6.5 cm) diameter. Chill in the fridge.

Skin the haddock and poach it for 10 minutes in the milk with the bayleaf and crushed black peppercorns. Lift it out and chop the flesh finely, then mix with the cream cheese. Stir in the whisky and season well.

Preheat the oven to Gas 6/400°F/200°C. Fill the tartlets with the haddock mixture, dotting the tops with tiny knobs of butter. Bake for 25 minutes until the pastry is cooked and the peaks of the mixture are browned.

Alternatively, fill the haddock and cheese mixture into four ramekins, put these into a bain marie and bake for 35 minutes in an oven preheated to Gas 4/350°F/180°C. Decorate with half a thin lemon slice.

Sardine Tartlets with Cream Cheese Pastry

This is a rather unusual pastry made with a very soft cream cheese dough containing a much smaller proportion of flour than usual. It is important to refrigerate it well before rolling out, or you will end up with a sticky mess.

Makes about 12

4½ oz (125 g) tin sardines in oil
1 egg
1 tbsp lemon juice
pinch curry powder
seasoning
1 tbsp fresh chopped parsley

Pastry
3 oz (85 g) soft margarine
3 oz (85 g) low-fat cream cheese
3 oz (85 g) white flour

Mix the cream cheese and soft margarine together in a large bowl, then stir in the sifted flour. When the flour has coated and mixed in with the rest enough to handle, pick it up and lightly knead to a soft dough. Refrigerate for 45–60 minutes.

Hardboil the egg. Drain and mash the sardines and mix them with the lemon juice, curry powder, seasoning and chopped parsley. Shell and finely chop the egg and add this.

Roll out the dough and cut out circles using a 3½ inch (9 cm) crinkled cutter. With the pastry, line a tray of 12 straight-sided tartlet tins, each 2½ inches (6.5 cm) diameter. Fill each with a teaspoon or two of the sardine mixture and bake in an oven preheated to Gas 7/425°F/220°C for about 15 minutes, until the pastry is cooked. Serve hot.

Marinated Kipper Fillets

I call this 'poor man's smoked salmon' because although nothing, of course, can compare with the exquisite taste of the real thing, kippers have a similar oily texture and can be very good indeed prepared in this way. When cut into paper-thin slices and attractively garnished, this makes the most of a very British fish.

Be sure to choose kippers that aren't heavily impregnated with artificial dye. Thanks to recent public awareness of the effects of food dyes and additives, more smoked fish is appearing on the market with no artificial colouring or preservatives.

Serves 4

2 double kipper fillets
1 medium onion
1 clove garlic (optional)
black peppercorns
3 tbsp olive oil

1 tbsp fresh lemon juice
1 tbsp wine vinegar
4 bayleaves
mustard and cress
4 lemon wedges

Put the unskinned kipper fillets in a deep dish where they fit snugly. Chop the onion and garlic and crush the peppercorns, sprinkle these over both fish. (You can halve the kippers into single fillets if they don't fit in your dish, but leave the skin on.) Pour the oil, lemon juice and vinegar over the fish and sprinkle with the bayleaves, broken into pieces.

Leave for a minimum of 6 hours (you can marinate them for up to 3 days if you like), turning and basting as often as you remember. After this time, take the fillets out of the dish, scrape off the marinade and pat dry with kitchen paper. Using a sharp, flexible filleting knife, slice the kippers as you would smoked salmon, in almost horizontal strokes towards the tail. Your knife *must* be razor sharp.

Arrange the small slices overlapping neatly on a serving plate, sprinkle with half a punnet of mustard and cress, garnish with the lemon wedges and serve with brown bread and butter, with a pepper grinder for people to add their own seasoning. A crisp salad of lettuce and radicchio or watercress goes well with this.

Anchovy with Bean Salad

Haricot beans mixed with salty anchovy in a pungent French dressing is a popular dish in many brasseries in France, evoking for me memories of strong Provençal flavours first tasted in the open air at Avignon. In this recipe I have added a lemony lentil purée, which serves as a bed for the white haricot beans and makes quite a substantial dish. The soaking of

Cod in Cider with Julienne of Vegetables (page 165)

the beans should be started the day before, although you can cheat by using a 14 oz (390 g) tin of haricots.

Serves 4

8 oz (225 g) dried haricot beans
2 x 1¾ oz (50 g) tins anchovies
a little milk (optional)
8 oz (225 g) brown or green
   lentils
juice of 1 lemon
½ onion
1 clove garlic
2 tbsp fresh chopped parsley
4 tomatoes

French dressing
4 tbsp olive oil
2 tbsp white wine vinegar
salt
black pepper
¼ tsp French mustard

Soak the haricot beans overnight in cold water, then drain and simmer them in unsalted water for 1½–2 hours (depending on their age and quality), or in a pressure cooker for 15–20 minutes at H Pressure. (Cooking pulses in salted water means they take longer to soften.) Drain and cool.

Soak the anchovy fillets in a little milk for an hour to remove some of the saltiness if you prefer. Wash the lentils and simmer them for 45 minutes until soft and just beginning to disintegrate — they don't need any preliminary soaking. Drain them and purée in a food processor with the juice of a lemon. Spread this purée over a round serving plate, leaving about 2 inches (5 cm) of plate showing round the edge.

Make the French dressing. Drain and halve the anchovy fillets. Finely chop the onion and mix it with the haricot beans, anchovy, crushed garlic and parsley. Turn this well in the French dressing and taste for seasoning. Pile it all up on top of the lentil purée, arrange quartered tomatoes round the edge and serve with warm French bread.

Do not put the anchovy mixture on top of the purée until shortly before serving, as the French dressing will seep on to the plate and spoil the appearance of the dish.

Monkfish with Sweet Pepper Pasta Sauce (page 91) and Smoked Trout Pâté with Smoked Salmon (page 118)

Main Courses

Fish Balls in Lemon Sauce

The method used for making fish balls is just like that for meat balls. However, since the flavour is more delicate, it is better (and healthier) to poach them in a little fish stock and white wine, rather than deep-fry them. The fishballs can be prepared in advance (even frozen), but the sauce should be done at the last minute.

Serves 4

1 lb (450 g) haddock fillet	1 pint (550 ml) fish stock
1 oz (30 g) dry white breadcrumbs	1 glass dry white wine
1–2 tbsp milk	
½ large onion	**Sauce**
2 tbsp fresh chopped parsley	½ pint (300 ml) fish stock
1 level tsp ground cumin	(using poaching liquid)
1 level tsp ground coriander	2 egg yolks
1 egg white	juice of 1 lemon
seasoning	1 dsp cornflour

Skin the filleted fish. Soak the breadcrumbs in the milk. Chop the onion very finely in a food processor, add the fish in chunks, the parsley, cumin and coriander and season well. Blend together. Squeeze the soaked breadcrumbs well to get rid of any excess milk. Transfer the fish to a mixing bowl and, using your fingers, incorporate the breadcrumbs thoroughly. Add the egg white, mix well and then roll the pieces of paste into walnut-sized balls in your hands.

Heat about 1 pint (550 ml) fish stock with the white wine in a saucepan. Drop the fish balls in and poach gently for about 5 minutes. Lift out and keep them warm in the oven, covered, while you make the sauce.

Reduce the poaching liquid to ½ pint (300 ml) by boiling it fast. (Strain and return it to the pan if it has bits of fish ball in it.) Allow to cool slightly. Add 2 egg yolks and the lemon juice, beaten together. Heat through but do not allow to boil or the eggs will scramble. Dissolve the cornflour in 3 tbsp cold water, pour into the sauce and heat, stirring. As it comes back to just below boiling point the sauce will thicken beautifully.

Pour the sauce over the fish balls and serve with rice.

Russian Cod in Cherry and Red Wine Sauce

You may be turning your nose up already at the idea of cooking fish not in white, but red wine, and thinking cherries a rather odd fruit to use for making the sauce. But the combination is common in Russian and some East European cooking (think of Hungary's delicious cherry soup). The authentic dish calls for sour Morello cherries, but being unable to find these I tried it with ordinary ones and found the end-result delicious.

Serves 4

1½–2 lb (670–900 g) cod fillet
up to ½ pint (300 ml) milk
bayleaf
¼ onion, sliced
black pepper

Sauce
8 oz (225 g) dark cherries

½ oz (15 g) butter
½ pint (300 ml) fish stock
small pinch cinnamon
4 cloves
¼ pint (150 ml) red wine
2 level tbsp cornflour
seasoning

Skin the cod fillet and divide into 4 portions. Place it in a small flameproof casserole with enough milk just to cover it, and add the sliced onion, bayleaf and some black pepper. Set to one side.

Stone the cherries and chop them finely. Sweat them very gently in the butter in a saucepan for 5 minutes and then pour on the fish stock, add the cinnamon and cloves and bring to simmering point. Cover and cook gently for 10 minutes. Half-way through the cooking time, put the casserole containing the fish over a medium heat and bring the milk to poaching temperature, then leave it to cook for 10 minutes.

Remove the cloves from the cherry sauce and pour in the red wine. Simmer very gently for 5 minutes, then stir in the cornflour dissolved in 3 tbsp cold water. As it heats through the sauce will thicken, but do not allow it to boil. Test for seasoning.

The fish should now be ready, so remove it from the milk, drain well and serve with the cherry sauce poured over. Plain boiled potatoes go well with this dish, as they can be used to mop up the delicious sauce.

Cod in Cider with Julienne of Vegetables

A simple everyday dish which is prepared from ingredients which are easily available. All you need to accompany it is a baked potato.

Serves 4

4 cod steaks	seasoning
1 lb (450 g) carrots	bayleaf
2 medium leeks	pinch thyme
1½ oz (45 g) butter	½ oz (15 g) white flour
½ pint (300 ml) dry cider	

Peel the carrots and cut them into julienne (matchsticks) about 2 inches (5 cm) long. If you have the julienne attachment for a food processor, this takes seconds, but you can do them quite easily by hand. Do the same with the leeks (which is much quicker), but wash them afterwards in a sieve under cold running water to remove any grit.

Melt 1 oz (30 g) of the butter in a flameproof casserole and add the vegetables — they should about half-fill the casserole. Sweat them in the butter over a gentle heat for not more than 5 minutes. Place the cod steaks on top, side by side, and pour over the cider. Season well, add a bayleaf and the thyme. Bring to the boil, cover and simmer 5–10 minutes until the steaks are cooked.

Remove the fish. Put the vegetables on a serving dish and keep warm. Quickly skin and bone the cod steaks, lay them on top of the vegetables and keep warm. Make a roux in a small saucepan with the rest of the butter and the flour. Strain on the cider and stir till well blended. Pour over the fish and vegetables and serve.

Cod Portugaise

If you are one of those people who hates dealing with fish on the bone at the table, use cod fillet for this dish. If you choose cod steaks, which are a little cheaper, buy ones that aren't too big — about 7 oz (195 g).

Serves 4

4 cod steaks or 1½ lbs (550 g) fillet	1 tbsp olive oil
1 green pepper	14 oz (390 g) tin tomatoes
1 red pepper	pinch rosemary
1 medium onion	pinch thyme
1 large clove garlic	1 tbsp fresh chopped parsley
	black pepper

Slice the onion and de-seed and slice the peppers. Heat the oil in a saucepan and sauté the sliced vegetables with the crushed garlic for

5 minutes. Add the tomatoes and herbs and season well with black pepper. Simmer, uncovered, for 15 minutes without stirring.

If you are using cod fillet, skin it and cut into 4 portions. Pour half the sauce into a shallow ovenproof dish, put the fish on top and cover with the remaining sauce. Bake for 10–15 minutes in an oven preheated to Gas 6/400°F/200°C until the fish is cooked. Sprinkle with the chopped parsley.

Serve with rice or new potatoes.

Red Peppers Stuffed with Curried Cod

Cod is especially suitable for this dish, since it has a firm texture and robust taste which will not be overwhelmed by the curry sauce. Other white fish such as monkfish, for example, could be used instead. You can stuff the blanched peppers in advance, so that all that remains is to bake them in the oven for half an hour. Try and use the spices below if you have them — a tablespoon of curry powder is an acceptable, but inferior, substitute.

Serves 4

1¼ lb (550 g) cod fillet
4 medium-large red peppers
½ medium onion
2 tbsp sunflower oil
1 tsp ground coriander
½ tsp ground cumin
¼ tsp each of ground ginger,
    turmeric and chilli powder

2 tsp tomato purée
1 tbsp wholemeal flour
juice of ½ lemon
1 glass white wine
¼ pint (150 ml) fish stock or water
seasoning
bayleaf

First make the curry sauce. Finely chop the onion and sauté it in the sunflower oil for a few minutes, then stir in the spices and tomato purée and fry for 30 seconds. Stir in the flour and add the wine, stock and lemon juice gradually, stirring until you have a smooth thick sauce. Put in the bayleaf, season, cover and simmer very gently for 15 minutes.

Meanwhile cut the stalk end off the peppers to form a lid. With a small knife cut out the seeds from inside each pepper without piercing the skin. Put the peppers into a pan of water and bring to the boil, then simmer for 5 minutes. Drain and cool slightly.

Set the oven to Gas 4/350°F/180°C. Skin the fish fillet and cut it into small dice. Drop it into the sauce and stir till well coated and beginning to cook. Pack the fish into the peppers and put the lids on. Wrap each pepper well in greased silver foil and bake on a tray for 30 minutes.

Serve with brown rice and a cucumber raita (cucumber and yoghurt salad, with added chilli if desired).

Lemon and Prawn Stuffed Plaice

We once had a wonderful girl called Emma who came and cooked for us during a time of family crisis. One night she served up this dish, which lifted the humble frozen plaice to a gourmet dish and certainly went a long way towards lifting my spirits.

Serves 4

8 plaice fillets
3 oz (85 g) peeled prawns
2 slices day-old wholemeal bread
1 medium onion
1 oz (30 g) butter
½ lemon
1 dsp fresh chopped parsley
seasoning

Sauce
1 oz (30 g) butter
1 tbsp white flour
½ pint (300 ml) milk
2–3 tbsp dry white wine
1 oz (30 g) grated Parmesan cheese
1 oz (30 g) peeled prawns

Skin the plaice fillets. Remove the crusts from the bread and make it into crumbs in a food processor. Chop the onion and soften it in 1 oz (30 g) butter in a saucepan. In a bowl mix the breadcrumbs, onion, 3 oz (85 g) prawns, grated rind and juice of the half-lemon and the chopped parsley. Season well and spread the centre of each fillet with the mixture. Roll up and place in a shallow ovenproof dish.

Use a non-stick pan for the cheese sauce. Make a roux with the butter and flour and then stir in the white wine and milk till smooth. Mix in 1 oz (30 g) prawns and the grated Parmesan, test for seasoning and pour over the rolled-up fillets. Bake covered with silver foil, in an oven preheated to Gas 4/350°F/180°C, for 30–35 minutes. If you wish you can sprinkle the top with breadcrumbs and grated cheese and uncover the dish 15 minutes before the end of cooking to allow it to brown.

Fish in Pastry Pillowcases

Easy to prepare, these golden pastry parcels stuffed with a succulent mixture of cod and spinach make a good supper dish. Serve with fresh vegetables and you'll find this filling enough without having to cook potatoes as well. Haddock can be used instead of cod.

Serves 4

1–1¼ lb (450–550 g) cod fillet
2 x 7½ oz (210 g) packets
  puff pastry
8 oz (225 g) fresh spinach or 4 oz
  (110 g) frozen leaf spinach

pinch freshly grated nutmeg
black pepper
1 beaten egg

Skin the cod fillet and divide it into 4 pieces, weighing not more than
5 oz (140 g) each. Set aside. Wash the spinach well and snap off the
stalks, putting the leaves in a pan without any additional water. Cook
them for 5 minutes until most of the water has evaporated and the
spinach is much reduced in size. Drain it well, pressing it between two
plates or against the side of the colander to remove all excess water.
Chop and season with black pepper and nutmeg. (If you are using frozen
spinach, defrost it over a gentle heat, evaporate all the water and then
chop and season it.)

Cut the two pastry slabs in half across their width and roll out each
piece into a rectangle about 5 x 8 inches (13 x 20 cm). Place a piece of
cod in the middle and pile some spinach on top. You may need to fold
the fish, in which case sandwich some spinach in the middle as well.
Brush round the pastry edges with water.

Fold one of the longer pastry sides over its opposite, brushing with
water where they meet. Press lightly to seal. On the shorter sides, pinch
the edges together to form a small flap, resembling the edging on a frilly
pillowcase. Repeat with the other pieces of fish. Brush each parcel with
beaten egg, and bake in a preheated oven (Gas 6/400°F/200°C) for 25–30
minutes until the pastry is golden brown.

You can prepare the parcels in advance and refrigerate them, but make
sure you return them to room temperature before cooking, or otherwise
lengthen the baking time by about 5 minutes.

Ring the changes by trying these other fillings, allowing the same
amount of fish per head (quantities serve 4):

Mushroom

8 oz (225 g) button mushrooms   1 tsp tomato purée
1 oz (30 g) butter   approx. 2½ fl.oz (75 ml) milk
1 level tbsp wholemeal flour

Slice the mushrooms and soften them in the butter in a small saucepan.
Stir in the flour and tomato purée to absorb the fat, then add enough
milk to bind the mixture together. Proceed as above.

Courgette and Orange

2 courgettes
grated rind of ½ orange
black pepper

Top and tail the courgettes and grate them. Mix them with the grated
orange rind and season with black pepper. You do not need to cook this
mixture before enclosing it in the pastry parcel.

Smoked Oyster Flan

This can be eaten hot or cold, but make sure that it is well cooked in the middle or the filling will be rather watery when you cut into it.

Serves 3–4

2 x 3¾ oz (105 g) tins smoked
  oysters
½ oz (15 g) butter
1 medium onion
2 rashers streaky bacon
¼ pint (150 ml) sour cream or
  5 oz (140 g) each of low-fat
  soft cheese and natural yoghurt

2 eggs
seasoning

Shortcrust pastry
6 oz (170 g) white flour
3 oz (85 g) butter or hard
  margarine
1–2 tbsp cold water

Make the pastry as shown on page 190 and line a 7–8 inch (18–20 cm) flan tin with it, preferably one with a removable bottom. Chill the pastry case for 30 minutes then bake it blind for 20 minutes in an oven preheated to Gas 6/400°F/200°C. Remember to remove the beans and greaseproof paper for the final 5 minutes.

    Meanwhile prepare the filling. Chop the onion and de-rind and dice the bacon. Sauté them in the butter in a small pan for about 5 minutes, then remove from the heat and stir in the drained smoked oysters, beaten eggs and sour cream (or cheese and yoghurt beaten together). Season and pour into the partly baked flan case.

    Cook in the oven at the same temperature for 10 minutes, then turn it down to Gas 4/350°F/180°C and bake a further 25–30 minutes until the filling is set and golden brown. Remove from the flan tin and serve.

Kipper and Black Olive Flan

Both kippers and black olives are fairly strong-tasting, so serve this with a simple salad and baked potatoes. Choose kippers containing no artificial dye — they may be more expensive, but they seem less salty and dried out than the others, apart from sparing your body the absorption of unnecessary chemicals.

Serves 3–4

8 oz (225 g) kipper fillets
2 eggs
up to ¼ pint (150 ml) single
  cream
black pepper
3 oz (85 g) black olives

a little milk

Pastry
6 oz (170 g) white flour
3 oz (85 g) butter or hard margarine
1–2 tbsp cold water

Make the pastry in a food processor or by hand. Roll it out and line a greased flan tin, about 7–8 inches (18–20 cm) diameter, reserving the leftover pastry and storing it in the fridge until later. Bake the flan case blind in an oven preheated to Gas 6/400°F/200°C for 25 minutes.

Skin the kipper fillets and slice them, arranging the slices in the bottom of the flan. Break the eggs into a measuring jug, beat them and add single cream until the total volume is 8 fl.oz (225 ml). Season with black pepper and pour over the kipper. Roll out the remaining pastry, cut four strips about ½ inch (1 cm) wide and arrange them, evenly spaced, across the flan. Trim the ends and press them down lightly. Stone the olives and arrange them evenly spaced in the gaps. Brush the pastry strips with a little milk, or some of the cream and egg mixture.

Bake the flan for 30 minutes at Gas 6/400°F/200°C until the filling is firm and the pastry strips cooked.

Curried Fish Croquettes

If you have them, individual spices are best used here, but curry powder will do. Check you have enough oil (sunflower) for deep-frying — if shallow-fried the croquettes often tend to split and do not come out so crisp.

Serves 4

1 lb (450 g) cod fillet	2 level tsp curry powder or pinch
1 pint (550 ml) court bouillon	each of cumin, coriander and chilli
½ oz (15 g) butter	1 tbsp flour
½ small onion	wholemeal flour, egg and breadcrumbs for coating

Skin the cod fillets and poach them in the court bouillon on top of the stove for 10 minutes. Remove and mash the fish well, or chop it finely in a food processor. Chop the onion very finely and cook it in the butter until soft. Stir in the curry spices and flour and cook a few minutes to make a paste. Add about 4 tbsp of the fish stock to make a really thick sauce and then stir in the fish. If it's very dry add a little more stock to bind, but don't overdo it or the mixture will be too sloppy to roll into shape.

Leave to go cold in the fridge, which will firm the mixture up. Then, on a floured board, roll it into 12 croquettes, each about 2½–3 inches (6.5–7.5 cm) long. Heat the oil ready for deep-frying (make sure it's really hot or the croquettes will absorb too much oil and be soggy). Flour, egg and breadcrumb the croquettes and deep-fry until golden brown.

Serve with a tartare sauce (see page 187).

Salmon Fishcakes

These freeze well, so it would be worth making double the quantity and storing them in the freezer for when you're pressed for time. A good everyday supper dish that is also popular with children.

Serves 4 (makes 8 fishcakes)

just over 8 oz (225 g) potatoes
8 oz (225 g) tin pink salmon
½ oz (15 g) butter
seasoning
1 tbsp fresh chopped parsley

1 large egg
1 oz (30 g) fine oatmeal
1 tbsp wholemeal flour
sunflower oil

Peel, boil and mash the potatoes, but do not add any milk when mashing them or the fishcakes will be rather sloppy. Drain the salmon and pick out any dark skin and the central bone. Melt the butter and mix it with the potatoes and flaked salmon, season well.

Stir in the parsley and enough of the beaten egg (half or less) to bind, but be careful not to add too much or the mixture will be too soft to handle satisfactorily. Put the rest of the egg on a plate and whisk it lightly with a fork.

Sprinkle the oatmeal on to another plate. Scatter the flour over the work surface and shape the mixture into cakes, dipping them first in the egg and then the oatmeal. If you do find the mixture is a bit soft, stir in 1 tbsp breadcrumbs, or you could chill it to harden up the butter. Each fishcake should be roughly the same diameter as a medium tin of tomatoes.

Either freeze uncovered on a tray and then pack into a container, or fry for about 10 minutes in the oil until golden brown. If you leave them for more than about 10 minutes without doing either, the oatmeal will absorb moisture from the fishcake and not provide the necessary crisp coating. Serve with a tomato sauce (see page 189).

You can cook the fishcakes from frozen without thawing them first, but allow a little extra time for the centres to cook through.

Salmon Mousse

Tinned salmon can make a surprisingly good mousse so long as you pay attention with the other ingredients. This may not look like a large quantity when you've finished making it, but it is fairly rich and can stretch to six portions if you are having another course. For a somewhat lighter mousse, substitute natural yoghurt for the double cream.

Serves 4–6

8 oz (225 g) tin pink salmon
½ pint (300 ml) milk
¼ onion
black peppercorns
bayleaf
1 tsp anchovy essence
½ tsp tomato purée
1 tbsp lemon juice

½ oz (15 g) butter
½ oz (15 g) white flour
4 tbsp double cream
seasoning
2 oz (55 g) melted butter
0.4 oz (11 g) sachet gelatine
2 egg whites
½ cucumber

Roughly chop the onion and crush the peppercorns. Put them in a small saucepan with the milk and the bayleaf and bring to the boil. Remove from the heat and leave for 10 minutes for the milk to absorb the other flavours. Strain and set to one side.

Meanwhile drain the tin of salmon, reserving the juice. Pick out any dark skin and the central bone and flake the fish in a fairly large bowl, mixing it with the anchovy essence, tomato purée and lemon juice. In a pan over a low heat make a roux with the butter and flour and add the strained milk, stirring until you have a smooth béchamel sauce. Stir in the cream and season well.

Mix 4 tbs of béchamel with the salmon (you may have some left over, but it is not practical to make a smaller quantity of sauce) and stir in the melted butter. Put the juice from the tin of salmon into a small saucepan with 1–2 tbsp water and sprinkle the gelatine over the surface. Leave until it has absorbed some of the liquid and swollen (this is known as sponging) and then warm it over a very gentle heat until the gelatine granules have completely dissolved. Pour into the salmon mixture and leave in the freezer for 10 minutes to cool quickly.

Stiffly beat the egg whites and fold them into the salmon mixture. Make sure you add the egg whites to the salmon and not vice-versa or you will knock the air out. (This is also why they should be folded together in a fairly large bowl.) Pour into a 1–1½ pint (550–850 ml) soufflé dish and leave to set in the fridge.

To serve, turn the mousse out on to a plate. Thinly slice the cucumber, using a mandolin if you have one, and decorate the top of the mousse and round the edge of the plate with cucumber slices.

Hot Haddock Mousse

This is an excellent cooked savoury mousse made from what would otherwise be rather unexciting frozen haddock. It has the added advantage of not spoiling if left in the oven for a while when you are late sitting down to eat. It can be prepared in advance up to the folding in of the egg whites. Unlike a classic soufflé, it doesn't rise much, so you don't need to leave much space between the mixture and the top of the dish.

Serves 4

1 lb (450 g) filleted haddock	4 tbsp single cream
1 pint (550 ml) court bouillon	2 tbsp fresh chopped parsley
4 tbsp milk	seasoning
1 oz (30 g) butter	2 tsp anchovy essence
1 tbsp white flour	a little sunflower oil
2 large eggs	

Skin the fish fillets and poach them in the court bouillon for 10 minutes. Lift out, reserving the stock, and mash well with a fork, or process for a few seconds in a food processor. Put the milk in a measuring jug and make it up to ¼ pint (150 ml) with some of the stock.

Make a roux with the butter and flour. Add the milk/stock gradually, stirring well until you have a smooth thick sauce. Cook over a gentle heat for a few minutes while you separate the eggs, putting the whites in a fair-sized bowl for whipping and mixing the yolks with the cream.

Remove the sauce from the heat and stir in the haddock, cream and yolks, parsley, seasoning and anchovy essence. Oil a 1½ pint (850 ml) soufflé dish and preheat the oven to Gas 3/325°F/170°C. Whip the egg whites stiffly, fold them into the fish mixture and empty into the soufflé dish. Set the dish in a roasting tin, surrounded by enough hot water to come about one-third of the way up the sides of the dish (filling it from a boiled kettle is the easiest method).

Bake in this bain marie for 1–1¼ hours until set. It is advisable to cover the mousse with greased silver foil until about 30 minutes before the end of cooking, or the top will over-brown.

Baked Tuna Loaf

Equally good served hot with tomato sauce, or cold with salad, this fish version of a meat loaf is very economical to make.

Serves 4–6

7 oz (195 g) tin tuna	½ oz (15 g) wholemeal flour
4 oz (110 g) frozen prawns	¼ pint (150 ml) milk
2 oz (55 g) dried wholemeal breadcrumbs	1 tsp anchovy essence
	black pepper
¼ pint (150 ml) dry white wine	1 tbsp fresh chopped parsley
½ oz (15 g) butter	a little sunflower oil

Defrost the prawns, pat them dry and mix with the drained and flaked tuna. Soak the breadcrumbs in the wine and stir them into the fish. In a saucepan make a roux with the melted butter and flour, then stir in the milk. Season it with anchovy essence and black pepper and cook until thick, then stir into the fish mixture, adding the parsley.

Lightly grease a 1 lb (450 g) loaf tin or terrine dish with a knob of margarine. Pack the fish mixture into it, cover with a double thickness of oiled silver foil, and bake on a tray in a preheated oven (Gas 5/375°F/ 190°C) for 45 minutes. If you are going to eat it cold, compress the fish loaf with weights or full tins for a few hours in the fridge before turning out on to a plate.

Sardine and Anchovy Pasta Sauce

A quick and easy sauce straight out of the storecupboard (although fresh ripe tomatoes are preferable if you have them to hand). You may not think, having cooked it, that the sauce will stretch to 4 people, but this is a cheap dish in the Italian style — a large steaming bowl of filling pasta with a little pungent sauce just coating the shapes.

Serves 4

1¾ oz (50 g) tin anchovies	6 medium tomatoes or 14 oz
2 x 4½ oz (125 g) tins sardines	(390 g) tin
in oil	4 tbsp red wine
2 tbsp olive oil	pinch thyme
½ small onion	black pepper
1 clove garlic	1 tbsp fresh chopped parsley
	12 oz (335 g) pasta spirals

Chop the onion finely and sauté it with the crushed garlic in the olive oil in a small saucepan for a couple of minutes. Drain the sardines and anchovies and cut them into 3 or 4 pieces. Chop the tomatoes. Add the fish and tomatoes to the pan with the red wine and thyme and season with black pepper. Half-cover and simmer for 10 minutes, stirring occasionally, while the pasta cooks.

Dish up the pasta, mix in the sauce and serve sprinkled with the chopped parsley. A green salad is all you need as an accompaniment.

Shellfish Pasta Sauce

This is a fish version of the classic meat bolognese sauce. All the ingredients can be found in the storecupboard or freezer, so it's the ideal dish to make when you have unexpected guests and no fresh fish in the house.

Serves 4

6 oz (170 g) frozen peeled prawns
3½ oz (105 g) tin smoked mussels
   or smoked oysters
1 medium onion
1 clove garlic
1 tbsp olive oil

14 oz (390 g) tin tomatoes
4 tbsp dry white wine
pinch dried thyme
pinch dried basil
seasoning
12 oz (335 g) pasta spirals or shells

Chop the onion and soften it in the olive oil in a non-stick saucepan with the crushed garlic. Add the tomatoes, wine, herbs and seasoning and simmer, covered, for 30 minutes over a gentle heat. Defrost and pat dry the prawns and drain the mussels. Add them to the sauce and simmer for 5 minutes. The sauce should be quite thick. If it is still rather runny boil it over a high heat uncovered, before adding the seafood, to reduce it to the right consistency to coat the pasta.

Serve poured over pasta spirals (tortiglioni) or shells (conchiglie), sprinkled with Parmesan if desired.

The Basics

Stocks

Court Bouillon

One of the major differences between cooking meat and fish is the time factor. Fish cooks in minutes, meat often in hours. While a simple meat casserole, made with cheap cuts, gives the meat plenty of time to absorb the flavours of the vegetables, herbs or wine which make up the sauce it is cooking in, this is not the case with fish.

Consequently, the first rule in fish cookery is to remember that the liquid a fish poaches in should already have the flavours cooked into it, so that the fish, when you add it, can immediately begin to absorb them. The most basic stock is a court bouillon, literally translated as a 'short broth'. You can easily make a large batch of this in advance and freeze it in half-pint tubs, but it actually takes little time or effort to prepare fresh.

Once used, it will have absorbed yet more flavour, this time from the fish it has been poaching. Don't throw it away therefore, but reduce it by fast boiling to concentrate the flavour, cool and freeze for use in a light soup or sauce.

The following recipe gives enough court bouillon to cook a piece of fish large enough for 4 or 6 people. If you are making a batch for the freezer, simply multiply up.

1 pint (550 ml) water	bayleaf
1 tbsp vinegar	parsley stalks
pinch salt	¼ small onion
1 tbsp crushed black peppercorns	½ stick celery (optional)

Put everything in a pan and bring to the boil. Simmer 20 minutes and then strain before use.

Fish Stock or Fumet

Most sauces and soup bases in fish cookery call for a stronger and fishier flavour than a court bouillon. Again, it is much quicker and easier to make a fish stock, or fumet as it is sometimes called, than a meat one.

Fish stock is made with trimmings of fish (head, bones, skins), plus water or an already-used court bouillon, and the usual flavourings of onion, seasoning and herbs (see above). Get in the habit of always asking your fishmonger for the trimmings of the fish he is filleting for you. Although most fishmongers pass on their fishbones to restaurants for stock, they will usually give or sell you for a nominal price any spare.

Sole bones are best, followed by any white fish. Oily fish like mackerel and herring do not produce very good stock. The shells of crabs, lobsters and even prawns produce an excellent base for shellfish soups. I consider it perfectly acceptable at home to keep the debris from cleared plates after you have served a dressed crab, boil it up (which sterilizes it) and then freeze it for a future crab soup base. Other families may be more fastidious.

It is impossible to give exact quantities, since the amount of liquid depends on the size of your saucepan and the amount of fish trimmings you are adding. The important thing is to cover all the fish bones to extract maximum flavour, so break them up if necessary and push down into the saucepan.

fish trimmings
water or court bouillon to cover
pinch salt
1 tbsp crushed black peppercorns
bayleaf

parsley stalks
½ medium onion
1 stick celery (optional)
glass white wine (optional)

Put everything into a medium-sized saucepan, bring to the boil and simmer 20 minutes. Do not overcook or the stock can become a bit gluey. If you strain this into a measuring jug, it saves time measuring it out while cooking.

Fish bones quickly go smelly in a rubbish bin. If you have a waste disposal, you should find the trimmings are now soft enough to be got rid of in this way (except for the vertebrae of some of the larger fish). Otherwise wrap well in newspaper before throwing away.

Béchamels

Béchamel is a classic savoury sauce, originally French but now used (and frequently misused) in many countries for coating fish and vegetables in particular, although it goes well with chicken too.

It is made by blending flavoured milk with a paste made from melted butter and flour, called a roux. It can be served alone or, once the basic béchamel is made, mixed with other ingredients to create the many béchamel-based sauces that form the backbone of classic fish cookery. Grated cheese, for example, may be added to create a sauce mornay, or you can include chopped onions (soubise), capers, herbs, mushrooms, lobster coral (cardinal), even Pernod. The list is long and varied.

Once you have learned the proportions and method, you can make it almost without thinking. On the other hand, a slip-shod approach or the attempt to take shortcuts in the making of béchamel sauce usually result in gluey, floury, lumpy imitations of the real thing. In England, a so-called béchamel coating overcooked cod has put generations off fish for life. The packets of white sauces offered as substitutes would make Louis de Béchamel, a financier at Louis XIV's court for whom the classic sauce was allegedly invented, turn in his grave.

The proportion of fat to flour, if using white flour, is usually equal, although the amount of fat can be slightly greater (up to ¼ oz/7 g). The milk should be added when warm or tepid, never boiling or granules will form. The important thing is to let the sauce cook long enough to break down the flour, both so that it thickens the sauce correctly, and so no over-floury taste spoils the sauce.

If you use wholemeal flour the final colour of the sauce will obviously
be altered and the flecks of bran will be visible, not that this matters to
many people. However, you will probably find that you need more
wholemeal flour to thicken the sauce in the same way as white flour
does, since the bran contains no thickening properties. Wholemeal flour
is much more variable than white — depending on the brand you use
you may need up to half as much again as you would using white. This
alters the consistency of the roux and unless you are an experienced cook
you may have to experiment at first, as with béchamel sauces proportions
and amounts are crucial.

One ounce (30 g) of white flour roughly equals a good rounded
tablespoon, and so I have given this measurement where appropriate to
save you time in weighing out the ingredients.

Basic Béchamel Sauce

These quantities make sufficient for coating 4–6 portions of fish. To
make a thinner sauce for pouring, use ¾ oz (20 g) each of flour and
butter to ½ pint (300 ml) milk. For a really thick béchamel to use as a
base for soufflés or for binding fishcakes, increase the amounts to 2 oz
(55 g) each, or cook for longer to reduce the amount of liquid.

½ pint (300 ml) milk	blade of mace
2–3 slices of onion	1 oz (30 g) butter
6–8 black peppercorns	1 oz (30 g) flour (1 tbsp)
1 small bayleaf	seasoning

Crush the peppercorns with a rolling-pin in the folded-over corner of a
tea towel and add to a small saucepan with the milk, onion and bayleaf.
Bring to the boil and then turn the heat down very low, so the milk is
not even simmering. Leave it to infuse for 10 minutes, allowing the
flavourings to permeate the milk, then strain into a jug.

Take a small heavy-bottomed saucepan, non-stick if you wish, and
melt the butter in it. Do not allow it to get too hot and start sizzling.
Add the flour all at once, off the heat, and stir well, then return to the
heat and cook gently for about 2 minutes. The paste, or roux, should be
fairly liquid, about the consistency of mustard. If it is too stiff add a tiny
bit more butter.

Cool the roux slightly, then gradually add the warm flavoured milk,
stirring continually. At first the milk will immediately be absorbed into
the roux, but keep adding and stirring and soon you will have the
blended smooth sauce you are looking for. Continue to cook gently for at
least 5–10 minutes, test for seasoning and use as required.

Cheese Sauce (Mornay)

Parmesan or Gruyère cheese are the best for this but many cooks in rural England have to make do with Cheddar. Whatever the cheese, to avoid lumps forming, use a fine grater. A pinch of dry English mustard is often added, but when making sauce mornay for fish dishes, I prefer to add a dash of anchovy essence.

½ pint (300 ml) basic béchamel   2–3 oz (55–85 g) grated Parmesan,
   (see above)   Gruyère or mature Cheddar
dash anchovy essence

Make the basic béchamel as in the previous recipe and simmer for the required 10 minutes. Then add the anchovy essence and grated cheese and stir in until the cheese has melted. Since cheeses like Gruyère and Cheddar will further thicken the sauce, you need to use a little less flour and butter, or a little more milk, to make the basic béchamel.

Mustard Sauce

This is an excellent accompaniment to grilled herrings and mackerel, as the sharp taste of the mustard cuts through the oiliness of these fish. The sour cream adds an extra tang.

½ pint (300 ml) basic béchamel   1 dsp French mustard (not the
   (see recipe above)   granular kind)
2 tbsp sour cream

Make the béchamel in the usual way (see above) then stir in the sour cream and mustard. Heat through, stirring, but do not allow it to boil or the cream may curdle.

Butter Sauces

Butter sauces, the best known of which is the hollandaise, are rich and not for everyday eating, but quite superb when served with a luxury fish like Dover sole, Scotch salmon or turbot. Unlike béchamels, which are thickened with flour, the consistency of a butter sauce (about that of double cream) is created by an emulsion of butter, egg yolks and vinegar.

Care is needed in making a butter sauce or it will curdle, and it should not be left unattended. Given these provisos, much of the mystique surrounding hollandaise and the variations deriving from it (béarnaise, mousseline, etc.), can be disregarded. It should not be attempted with anything other than butter, but the health-conscious can balance the calorie/cholesterol levels against the low fat content of the simply poached or steamed fish it accompanies.

As hollandaise is a rich sauce, only a small amount is needed. The following recipe stretches to serve 4 people.

Hollandaise Sauce

3 tbsp wine or tarragon vinegar   2 egg yolks (size 1 or 2 eggs)
1 slice lemon   4 oz (110 g) butter
1 small bayleaf   seasoning
6 black peppercorns

Put the vinegar, lemon, bayleaf and peppercorns into a small saucepan and boil until the liquid has been reduced to one tablespoonful. Strain, pour into a pudding basin that will fit over a saucepan and cool slightly. (Don't cheat and just start with 1 tbsp of vinegar, or you will not have the required concentration of flavour.)

Add the egg yolks to the vinegar and beat together. Place the bowl over a pan of just-simmering water. Cut the butter in about 8 pieces and add them one by one, beating with a wooden spoon or a small balloon whisk until each piece has melted before adding the next one. The water should not be allowed to boil or the egg yolks will start to scramble.

Continue beating until the sauce has thickened. It is the right consistency when, after you run your finger across the back of the wooden spoon, the line stays visible for some time. After testing for seasoning it should be served immediately in a warmed sauceboat.

If it curdles   Add a tablespoon of really hot water (have the kettle ready-boiled) and beat well. If this doesn't work, put a fresh yolk into a new bowl and add the curdled mixture little by little, over the pan of water, then proceed as before, using a little extra butter.

Quick Hollandaise

Modern technology in the form of the liquidizer and food processor now means you can make a virtually foolproof hollandaise. Melt the butter while the vinegar is reducing. Put the yolks in the machine, pour in the reduced vinegar with the motor running, then slowly add the hot melted butter until the sauce thickens. Test for seasoning and serve immediately in a warmed sauceboat.

Cucumber Sauce

This is made in the same way as the classic hollandaise, but uses 1 egg yolk and 1 whole egg to 3 oz (85 g) butter for a slightly lighter effect. The quantity of butter needed is also less, as the chopped cucumber makes up the bulk.

3 tbsp tarragon vinegar
small bayleaf
6 peppercorns
1 egg and 1 yolk

3 oz (85 g) butter
seasoning
squeeze lemon juice
½ cucumber, finely chopped

Make the basic sauce as above, adding the chopped cucumber and a squeeze of lemon juice after you have seasoned the sauce. Allow this to heat through before serving immediately in a warmed sauceboat.

Herb Sauce

basic hollandaise (see above)
1 level tbsp each of fresh chopped parsley, tarragon, chives and mint

Make the basic hollandaise as above and whisk in the fresh chopped herbs just before serving. This is excellent served with simply poached sole or a whole foil-baked salmon.

Mayonnaises

Mayonnaise is so easy to make at home that I fail to understand why anyone buys the commercial varieties, which are ruinously expensive and also too tart for many dishes. A mayonnaise is a straightforward emulsion of oil and egg yolks, with a little acid added in the form of wine vinegar or lemon juice. With a food processor or electric whisk it can be made in seconds and stored in a screwtop jar in the fridge for one or two weeks.

Mayonnaise goes very well with many fish dishes and with the addition of varying ingredients can itself assume many different forms.

Below I give the basic recipe and method. If you do not own the necessary machinery, you should follow the same method when making it by hand, using a small balloon whisk. Tie a twisted wet cloth around the very base of the bowl to hold it steady while you beat.

The type of oil you use depends on your taste, but it should be good quality. I find some olive oils too strong for mayonnaise and prefer to either mix olive oil with sunflower oil, or use just sunflower oil. Corn oil, which has a rather unpleasantly strong taste, is not suitable. Take the eggs out of the fridge about 20 minutes before starting, as if everything is not at room temperature the mayonnaise may curdle.

Basic Mayonnaise

Makes ½ pint/300 ml
2 size 2–3 egg yolks
pinch dry mustard
small pinch salt
½ pint (300 ml) oil (see above)

1 tbsp white wine vinegar or 2 tbsp lemon juice
1 tbsp hot water (optional)

Put the egg yolks into the machine with the mustard and salt and process for 30 seconds. Have the oil in a measuring jug and add it in a very thin trickle. (If doing it by hand, it should be just a few drops at a time.) After you have added nearly half, the mayonnaise will suddenly start to get thicker and stop making that sloppy sound as it whizzes round. You can now start adding the oil somewhat faster. Finish with the vinegar or lemon juice, and if you want to achieve a paler, creamier effect, add the hot water.

If it curdles   Empty the curdled mixture into another jug, start again with one fresh egg yolk, and gradually beat in the curdled mixture, then continue with the oil as usual. Curdling occurs if the oil is added too quickly, the oil or yolks are too cold, or the yolks are stale. The larger the amount you are making, the less it matters if you add a bit too much or too little oil.

Aioli (Garlic Mayonnaise)

Proceed as above, including 2–4 cloves of peeled, crushed garlic when you add the vinegar or lemon juice.

Tartare Sauce

Best known as an accompaniment to fish fried in breadcrumbs, tartare sauce also goes well with oily fish like smoked mackerel.

Proceed as above. When the mayonnaise is ready, add the following ingredients, finely chopped, to each ½ pint (300 ml) mayonnaise:

2 hardboiled eggs
3–4 small gherkins
¼ small onion

1 dsp fresh chopped parsley
1 tbsp chopped capers

Herb Mayonnaise

This mild, fresh-tasting mayonnaise goes well with delicate-flavoured cold fish like smoked trout, salmon trout or salmon.

Proceed as above, mixing in the following fresh herbs to each ½ pint (300 ml) mayonnaise:

1 tbsp finely chopped parsley
1 tbsp finely chopped chives

1 tbsp finely chopped tarragon

Remoulade

A sharp, picquant sauce especially suited to serving with cold shellfish.

Proceed as above, adding to each ½ pint (300 ml) mayonnaise:

2 tsp French mustard
1 tbsp chopped capers
1 tbsp fresh chopped tarragon

1 tbsp chopped gherkins
1 tbsp fresh chopped parsley
1 tsp anchovy essence

Mossbank Mayonnaise

This is technically not a true mayonnaise, since it uses whole eggs. This makes the sauce much runnier as well as somewhat lighter. It should be made in a liquidizer.

The recipe came from a friend's mother living on the Isle of Skye, where she concocts memorable meals with the somewhat limited variety of ingredients that are available locally. It became a favourite in our family and we called it after the name of her house.

2 whole size 3 eggs
2 tbsp wine vinegar
large pinch salt
1 level tsp mustard powder
1 tbsp chopped fresh herbs or
   1 tsp dried

1 level tsp castor sugar
1 tsp lemon juice
½ clove garlic (optional)
pinch paprika
½ pint (300 ml) sunflower oil

Put everything except the oil into the liquidizer and switch to top speed. Process for 1 minute. Switch to a medium speed and slowly add the oil in a thin trickle, increasing the amount as the mayonnaise thickens. This will take about 1½–2 minutes, but will not end up as thick as a conventional mayonnaise.

Pour into a screwtop jar and keep in the fridge.

Miscellaneous Sauces

French Dressing

Everybody has their own way of making French dressing. The main thing is not to get it so sharp it is acidic, but on the other hand you don't want it so oily that it leaves an unpleasant coating in the mouth. I use one part vinegar to 3 of oil and find shaking everything up in a tightly-lidded screw-top jar both creates a good emulsion and provides a handy storage container.

½ tsp French mustard
   (non-granular)
3 turns of the black pepper grinder

pinch salt
1 tbsp white wine vinegar
3 tbsp olive oil

First mix the mustard and seasoning together with the vinegar — this is important, because mustard does not dissolve properly in oil, and you will end up with lumps of it if you mix the whole lot together at once. Add the oil and whisk well if in a bowl, or shake in a securely fastened screw-top jar. Do not keep for more than a week before making fresh.

Basic Tomato Sauce

Once mastered, you will use this again and again with all types of dishes. The main thing to remember is that you should let it cook for at least 20 minutes to obtain the right consistency, so put it on to simmer while you prepare the main course. You could make up large quantities and freeze them in individual tubs, but don't store them for too long as the garlic taste will spoil.

1 tbsp olive oil	14 oz (390 g) tin peeled tomatoes
1 large clove garlic	pinch thyme
½ medium onion	pinch basil
1 level tbsp flour (white or wholemeal)	2 tbsp red wine (optional)
	bayleaf
1 tsp tomato purée	seasoning

Heat the oil in a non-stick saucepan and sauté the chopped onion and crushed garlic until soft but not browned. Stir in the flour and tomato purée and cook for about 30 seconds, then add the tomatoes, crushing them well with a spoon or potato masher. Add the herbs and wine and season well, then cover and leave over a gentle heat for 20 minutes minimum, stirring just once or twice.

Remove the bayleaf before using the sauce.

Rouille

A pungent thick sauce from the South of France, rouille is traditionally served with the hearty fish soup, bouillabaisse. However, you can also offer it as a dip for crudités and Mediterranean prawns, or even as a side sauce with a fish salad. Since the quantities are fairly small I find it easier not to use a food processor for this, but instead to turn back to the traditional mortar and pestle.

1 thick slice white bread	6 tbsp olive oil
1–2 fresh red chillies	pinch salt
2 cloves garlic	1–1½ tbsp fish stock

Remove the crusts from the bread and soak it in a little water. De-seed and chop the chilli finely (using 1 or 2, depending on taste), wearing rubber gloves or plastic bags to protect your hands from the juice. Peel and crush the garlic with the flat end of a table knife blade, mixed with a little salt to stop it slipping. Pound in the chopped chilli. Squeeze out any excess water from the bread and mix this in to the paste. Gradually add the oil, drop by drop, beating as if you were making mayonnaise. Beat in a little fish stock at the end.

Watercress Sauce

This is a classic sauce for serving with hot salmon or salmon trout dishes. Its bright green colour contrasts well with the pink flesh of the fish. The quantity below will serve 6 people. Use fish stock made from sole or salmon bones.

2 bunches watercress
2 oz (55 g) soft butter
2–3 inch (5–8 cm) piece cucumber
½ oz (15 g) white flour

½ pint (300 ml) fish stock
1 tsp anchovy essence
seasoning
squeeze lemon juice

Wash the watercress really well and cut off the stalks. Put it into boiling salted water and simmer just a few minutes until tender. Drain well and purée it in a food processor with 1½ oz (45 g) of the butter (or sieve it and beat in the butter by hand). Chop the cucumber very finely, either by hand or in the food processor, and simmer it for a few minutes in its own juice in a pan.

Make a roux with the rest of the butter and the flour, then gradually blend in the fish stock until you have a smooth sauce. Add the anchovy essence and simmer the sauce for 5–10 minutes. Drop in the watercress butter, bit by bit, beating each time before adding more. Do not allow the sauce to boil. When it is all incorporated, stir in the hot cucumber, season well and add a squeeze of lemon juice before serving.

Shortcrust Pastry

Commercial frozen or chilled puff pastry is so good that I really don't feel it is worth home cooks making their own. However, shortcrust pastry is easy to make yourself and very cheap. I include here two methods, one for those with a food processor and one for those doing it by hand.

If you prefer, you can use half white and half wholemeal flour, or 81 per cent wholemeal. Pastry made using just wholemeal flour tends to be rather more heavy and solid.

To line a 7–8 inch (18–20 cm) flan tin or cover a pie dish 8 inches (20 cm) long:

6 oz (170 g) plain white flour
3 oz (85 g) butter or hard margarine
1–2 tbsp ice-cold water

To line a 9–10 inch (23–25 cm) flan tin or cover a pie dish 11 inches (28 cm) long:

8 oz (225 g) plain white flour
4 oz (110 g) butter or hard margarine
2–3 tbsp ice cold water

Method One   Fit the double-bladed knife into your food processor and sift the flour into the bowl. This is to incorporate the maximum amount of air and make the end-result lighter. Add the butter or margarine cut into 6–8 pieces and switch the machine on for about 10–15 seconds, until the mixture resembles breadcrumbs. Add 1–2 tbsp of ice-cold water through the funnel with the machine running and process for another 30 seconds until you see the dough beginning to come away from the side of the bowl.

Remove from the bowl and knead by hand on a floured board until smooth. Chill for 30 minutes before using (this prevents the pastry from shrinking during cooking).

Method Two   Sift the flour into a large mixing bowl and drop in the butter, cut into 6–8 pieces. Holding an ordinary table knife in each hand, cut the butter into the flour as far as possible. Then with clean cool hands rub the flour and butter between your finger tips, lifting your hands out of the bowl and letting the 'breadcrumbs' fall back in. Add the water and knead with one hand until smooth. Chill for 30 minutes before using.

It is important for the butter, your hands and the kitchen to be cool when making pastry by hand, or the butter will start to soften and not mix in properly.

Glossary of Cooking Terms

Bain marie   A large pan of hot water in which you place a dish either to be kept hot or to cook. A big roasting tin is ideal. It is easiest and safest to place the dish to be cooked (e.g. a mousse or terrine) in the bain marie first, put this into the preheated oven and then half-fill the pan with boiling water from a kettle. Cooking with a bain marie prevents the outside of a delicate dish like a mousse from becoming overdone.

Bake blind   To cook a pastry case before adding the filling. Line the flan or pie dish with pastry, line this with greaseproof paper and fill with dried haricot or other beans kept especially for baking blind. Remove the beans and paper 5 minutes before the end of cooking time. Baking blind gives a crisper final pastry.

Blanch   To put vegetables, meat or citrus rind into boiling water, return it to a simmer and partly cook for a very short time, then drain under cold water to set the colour. Blanching is also used to loosen the skins of tomatoes, etc., for peeling.

Bouquet garni   A bundle of herbs and spices, tied in a muslin bag and put into a dish to flavour it while cooking. The bag is then lifted out. It should contain a bayleaf, a sprig of thyme (or dried thyme) and a couple of parsley sprigs. Other ingredients like citrus peel, peppercorns, etc. can be added at will.

Court bouillon   An already-flavoured liquid in which fish is cooked. See recipe on page 179.

Fold in   To blend two substances together, using a wide spatula or large tablespoon. You should run the spatula round the edge of the bowl before drawing it down across the centre, thus literally folding the sauce or whatever over on itself.

Infuse   To leave herbs and spices in a hot liquid to extract their flavours before using the strained liquid in a recipe.

Julienne (of vegetables)   A term used to describe vegetables cut into matchstick-strips, usually used for a garnish, but sometimes as part of a dish.

Marinade (noun)   A mixture of liquid and spices or herbs in which you leave a piece of fish or meat to absorb some of the flavours (and in the case of meat and game, to tenderize), before cooking. Liquids which can be used include oil, vinegar, citrus juice, wine and yoghurt.

Marinade (verb)   To leave in a marinade. (Alternative spelling: marinate.)

Poach   To cook in a liquid that is barely simmering, more like just shuddering, either in the oven or on top of the stove, uncovered.

Reduce   To concentrate the flavours of a liquid by rapid boiling, so that the excess water is evaporated to give a stronger flavour to the sauce/ soup/stock.

Roux   A cooked paste made from fat (usually butter or margarine) and flour. It is used as a base for thickening sauces or soups. White flour is easier to work with and tends to make a thicker roux, but wholemeal can be used.

Sauté   To cook food in oil, or solid fat like butter, over a fairly high heat, turning the food frequently until evenly browned.

Skim   To remove the scum which rises to the top when a stock first comes to the boil. A perforated metal spoon is the best utensil, since it catches the bits but lets the liquid drain back.

Sweat   To soften by cooking very gently without browning, either in fat or in the food's own juices, in a covered pan.

Whisk   To beat air into cream or egg whites, thus greatly increasing their volume and making them lighter. An electric or hand whisk can be used, but if using an electric one, move it around a lot and use a large bowl to allow the maximum amount of air to be incorporated.

Imperial-Metric Conversion

I have made these as precise as possible. All metric weights are to the nearest few grams, but for measurement of liquids, particularly large amounts, the conversions are more approximate.

Weights

1 oz	30 g	10 oz	280 g	1¾ lb	785 g
2 oz	55 g	11 oz	310 g	2 lb	900 g
3 oz	85 g	12 oz	335 g	2½ lb	1.1 kg
4 oz	110 g	13 oz	365 g	3 lb	1.35 kg
5 oz	140 g	14 oz	390 g	3½ lb	1.55 kg
6 oz	170 g	15 oz	420 g	4 lb	1.8 kg
7 oz	195 g	1 lb	450 g	4½ lb	2 kg
8 oz	225 g	1¼ lb	550 g	5 lb	2.25 kg
9 oz	250 g	1½ lb	670 g		

1 ounce = 28 g   1 kilo = 2 lb 3 oz (2.2 lb)

Liquids

⅛ pint (2½ fl.oz)	75 ml	1¼ pints	600 ml
¼ pint (5 fl.oz)	150 ml	1½ pints	850 ml
½ pint	300 ml	1¾ pints	1 litre
¾ pint	425 ml	2 pints (1 quart)	1.1 litres
1 pint	550 ml		

Imperial measurements still found in some recipe books include fluid ounces and gills:
1 pint = 20 fl.oz   1 gill = ¼ pint

Oven Temperatures

Individual ovens vary in temperature, particularly if they are getting on in age. Only you can know how accurate yours is. Remember that in conventional ovens the temperature is hottest at the top, and convection ovens, where a fan creates an even temperature, are usually a little hotter than a normal model.

You should always preheat your oven before putting a dish in — this takes about 10–15 minutes. Cooking times given in this book are based on a preheated oven.

Gas Mark	Fahrenheit	Celsius	
¼	225°	110°	Very cool
½	250°	130°	
1	275°	140°	Cool
2	300°	150°	
3	325°	170°	Warm
4	350°	180°	Moderate
5	375°	190°	Moderately hot
6	400°	200°	
7	425°	220°	Hot
8	450°	230°	
9	475°	240°	Very hot

Index